Games to Play with Two-Year-Olds

Revised

Jackie Silberg

Illustrated by Joan Waites

Author Availability

Jackie Silberg is an acclaimed speaker, teacher, and trainer on early childhood development and music. You can arrange to have her speak, present, train, or entertain by contacting her through Gryphon House, 800.638.0928; 877.638.7576 (fax), PO Box 10, Lewisville, NC 27023 or at jsilberg@interserv.com.

Other Books by Jackie Silberg

Games to Play with Babies, 3rd Edition
Games to Play with Toddlers, Revised
125 Brain Games for Babies
125 Brain Games for Toddlers and Twos
300 Three Minute Games
500 Five Minute Games
The I Can't Sing Book
The Complete Book of Rhymes, Songs,
Poems, Fingerplays and Chants, with Pam Schiller

Bulk Purchase

Gryphon House books are available at special discount when purchased in bulk for special premiums and sales promotions as well as for fund-raising use. Special editions or book excerpts also can be created to specification. For details, contact the Director of Sales at Gryphon House.

Jackie Silberg

Games to Play with Two-Year-Olds

Over 40 New Games!

Illustrated by Joan Waites

gryphon house®, inc.
Lewisville, NC

Revised Edition

Dedication

This book is dedicated to the joy that children bring into our lives.

Acknowledgments

Thanks to Kathy Charner, the most wonderful editor an author can have. She makes the words come alive.

And to the Gryphon House family who works together to produce the beautiful product that you are looking at now.

Copyright

Copyright © 2002 Jackie Silberg
Published by Gryphon House, Inc.
PO Box 10, Lewisville, NC 27023
Visit us on the web at www.gryphonhouse.com

Illustrations: Joan Waites
Cover photograph: © Kate Kuhn, 2000

Reprinted September 2012

Library of Congress Cataloging-in-Publication Data

Silberg, Jackie, DATE–
     Games to play with two year olds / Jackie Silberg ; illustrations by Joan Waites. — Rev. ed.
     p. cm.
     Includes index
     ISBN 978-0-87659-235-9
     1. Games. 2. Early childhood education—Activity programs.
3. Motor ability in children. I. Title.
GV1203 .S538 2002
790.1'922—dc21   2002011978

Disclaimer

The publisher and the author cannot be held responsible for injury, mishap, or damages incurred during the use of or because of the activities in this book. The author recommends appropriate and reasonable supervision at all times based on the age and capability of each child.

Table of Contents

Games for Young Twos

Games for Middle Twos

Games for Older Twos

From the Author

When I was a new mother celebrating the joys of parenting, I remember many of my friends with older children telling me about the "terrible twos" and how my child would change into a "monster."

When my son turned two, I was expecting all kinds of negative behavior and instead found a delightful, curious, interesting, precious, and adorable two-year-old with a "joie de vivre."

Was my son different? Not one bit!! The myth prevails but the real truth is that a two-year-old child is a joy and wonder. "No," "I can't," and "I want to do it myself" need love and support as your two-year-old struggles for independence.

Permitting your child to take initiative and to be assertive is one of the greatest gifts that you can give him or her.

How lucky you are to have a two-year-old!!

Guidelines for Growth

While each child's development will be individual and unique, the following skills are those that two-year-olds will likely develop before age three.

Motor, Auditory and Visual Skills
Likes to listen to the same story over and over
Develops enough eye-hand coordination to copy a line
Hops on one foot
Walks up and down stairs placing one foot on each stair
Runs freely
Uses scissors with one hand to cut paper
Jumps through a plastic hoop
Slides down a slide
Older twos can ride a tricycle
Jumps and lands with feet apart or with one foot
     in front of the other
Marches
Balances on a beam
Develops right or left handedness
Jumps from various heights
Follows simple directions
Matches six basic colors
Responds to music and rhythm by swaying and bending knees

Language and Cognitive Skills
Talks to self and to dolls
Understands and stays away from common dangers
Repeats part of a nursery rhyme or joins in
Understands the concept of one
Takes things apart for the purpose of learning
Groups things together by color, form, or size
Uses short sentences to convey simple ideas
Takes apart and puts things together purposefully
Understands in, out, and under

Knows that different activities happen at different times of the day

Expresses feelings, desires, and problems verbally

Remembers and names objects absent for a short time

Identifies objects by their use

Is developing a vivid imagination

Begins to use pronouns

Constantly asks the names of objects

Uses plurals of words

Self-Concept Skills

Finds own play area of activity

Likes to help parents around the house

Puts on own coat and shoes (can't tie or button)

Feeds self using a fork and spoon and glass

Values playmates and friends

Feeds himself or herself

Drinks from a cup

Locates and names body parts

Sings part of a song

Brushes teeth

Puts together more complex puzzles

Likes talking on the phone

Enjoys going on excursions with an adult

Gives full name when asked

Refers to self by name

Gets drink without help

Shows pride in clothing

Helps put things away

Starts make-believe play

Enjoys naming possessions of others, telling to whom they belong

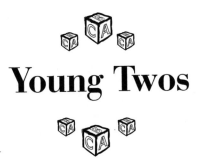

Young Twos

Animal Moves

- Cut out pictures of familiar animals from magazines.

- Glue each picture on a separate sheet of construction paper or poster board to create animal cards.

- Show the animal cards to your child and discuss each one. Talk about what the animal says and how the animal moves.

- Demonstrate how the animal moves and encourage your child to try to do it, too. Use exaggerated movements so that your two-year-old can better understand the size of the steps. For example, an elephant would take very slow, lumbering steps, and a kitty might take very quick and light steps.

- Put all the animal cards on a table. Ask your child to pick one card. Tell her the name of the animal she selected and ask her to move like that animal.

Here Is a Bunny

- Look at pictures of rabbits and bunnies with your child.

- Try hopping like a bunny and sniffing like a bunny.

- Pretend to be a bunny and eat a bunny lunch of carrots.

- Recite the following poem and perform the actions:

> *Here is a bunny with ears so funny. (hold up your pointer*
> *and middle finger)*
> *And here is his home in the ground. (cup your other hand)*
> *A noise he hears and he pricks up his ears, (move your two*
> *fingers that are standing up)*
> > *And jumps to his home in the ground. (dive your*
> > *fingers into your cupped hand)*

Wake Up!

- Talk about the different insects or animals that your child knows and the sounds that they make.

- Pretend that you and your child are bees. Make a buzzing sound and fly around the room.

- Now say that it is time for all the little bees to go to sleep.

- Close your eyes and pretend to be sleeping.

- Say to your child, "Wake up, little bee." Take a deep breath in, and then breathe out with a buzzing sound. Encourage your child to imitate you.

- Get up and buzz around the room again.

- Each time you play this game, make a different animal sound. The fun part will be taking a deep breath and exhaling with an animal sound.

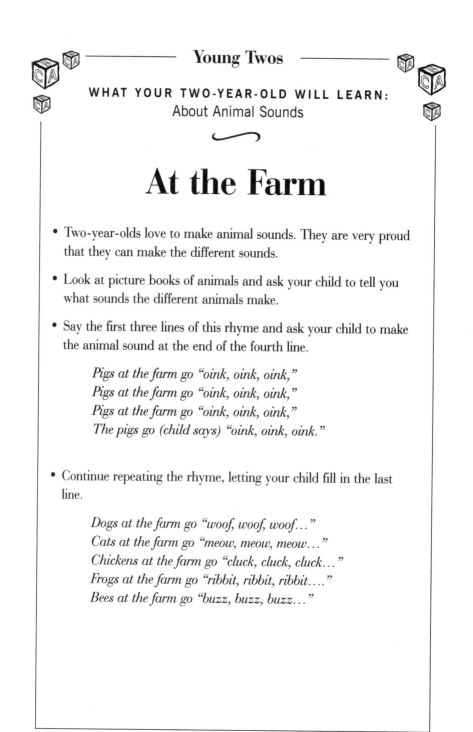

At the Farm

- Two-year-olds love to make animal sounds. They are very proud that they can make the different sounds.

- Look at picture books of animals and ask your child to tell you what sounds the different animals make.

- Say the first three lines of this rhyme and ask your child to make the animal sound at the end of the fourth line.

  Pigs at the farm go "oink, oink, oink,"
  Pigs at the farm go "oink, oink, oink,"
  Pigs at the farm go "oink, oink, oink,"
  The pigs go (child says) "oink, oink, oink."

- Continue repeating the rhyme, letting your child fill in the last line.

  Dogs at the farm go "woof, woof, woof..."
  Cats at the farm go "meow, meow, meow..."
  Chickens at the farm go "cluck, cluck, cluck..."
  Frogs at the farm go "ribbit, ribbit, ribbit...."
  Bees at the farm go "buzz, buzz, buzz..."

WHAT YOUR TWO-YEAR-OLD WILL LEARN:
About Animal Sounds

What Does It Say?

- Place the animal cards from "Animal Moves" (page 15) in various locations throughout the room.

- Tell your child that you are going to look for animals. Hold her hand and start walking to the places where you have put the cards. When you can see one of the cards, say:

  I see a _____ (name of animal), what does it say?
  What does it say?
  What does it say?
  I see a _____ (name of animal), what does it say?
  Tell me, what does it say?

- On the last line, "Tell me, what does it say?" pick up the card and make the animal sound.

How Do You Move?

- Pick three animals that your child knows. A book with pictures of these animals is a helpful aid for this game.

- Look at a picture of the chosen animal, such as a frog, and talk about its color, size, and how it moves.

- Get down on the floor and show your child how a frog moves. If she already knows, that's even better! It makes the game more fun.

- Continue with the next animal. Playing this game will develop your child's language and develop her motor skills.

- Other animals that you can use are wiggling worms, hopping rabbits, galloping ponies, slithering snakes, creeping mice, and pouncing kittens.

- And don't forget how you move!

Show Me How You...

- This game helps your child follow directions by encouraging her to listen to what you say.

- Start each direction with "Show me how you...." and continue the sentence.

- This game can get silly, and if it does, your two-year-old will love it.

- Say and do each action so that your child can imitate you.
    - Show me how you touch your head to your shoulder.
    - Show me how you touch your ear to the chair.
    - Show me how you touch the floor.
    - Show me how you touch your ankles.
    - Show me how you touch my neck.

- Praise your child each time she performs an action correctly.

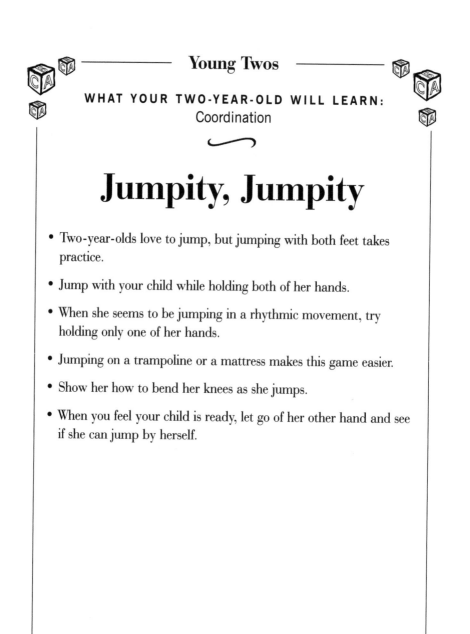

Jumpity, Jumpity

- Two-year-olds love to jump, but jumping with both feet takes practice.

- Jump with your child while holding both of her hands.

- When she seems to be jumping in a rhythmic movement, try holding only one of her hands.

- Jumping on a trampoline or a mattress makes this game easier.

- Show her how to bend her knees as she jumps.

- When you feel your child is ready, let go of her other hand and see if she can jump by herself.

Streamers

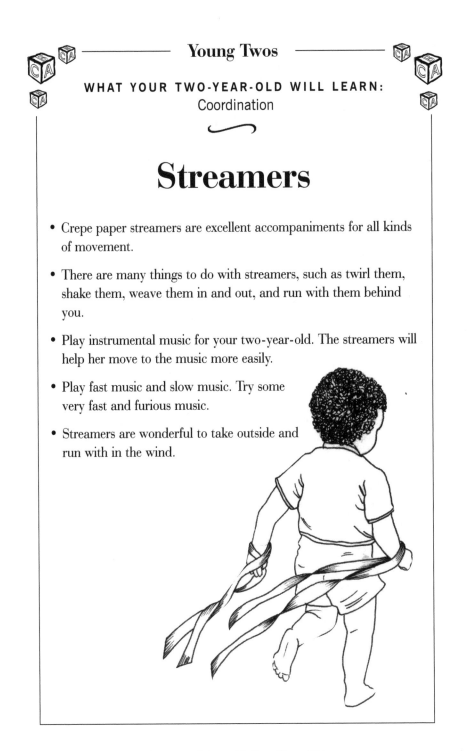

- Crepe paper streamers are excellent accompaniments for all kinds of movement.

- There are many things to do with streamers, such as twirl them, shake them, weave them in and out, and run with them behind you.

- Play instrumental music for your two-year-old. The streamers will help her move to the music more easily.

- Play fast music and slow music. Try some very fast and furious music.

- Streamers are wonderful to take outside and run with in the wind.

Andy Spandy

- This is a favorite movement game for two-year-olds. It is quick and action oriented.

- Recite the poem and do the actions.

    Andy Spandy, sugar candy, I pop down.
    Andy Spandy, sugar candy, I pop up.
    Andy Spandy, sugar candy, I pop in.
    Andy Spandy, sugar candy, I
        pop out.

- This poem is very good for language development because many words are repeated, which may encourage your child to say them.

- Instead of using the word "pop," say hop, jump, or any other word that occurs to you.

One, Two, Ready, Run

- Two-year-olds have so much energy. Running is one of their favorite activities.

- Play this game outdoors where you can run freely.

- Take three scarves of different colors and tie them to different objects such as trees or a fence. Make sure each object is running distance from the others.

- Say to your child, "One, two, ready, run!" Run to the tree.

- When you have reached the tree, say, "One, two, now I'm done."

- Repeat the same word pattern as you run from one object to another.

- If your two-year-old is interested in colors, identify the scarf you are running towards by its color. "Let's run to the blue scarf."

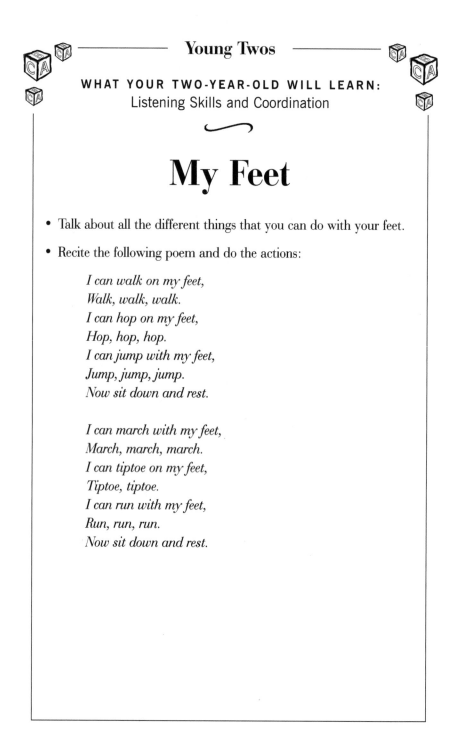

WHAT YOUR TWO-YEAR-OLD WILL LEARN:
Listening Skills and Coordination

My Feet

- Talk about all the different things that you can do with your feet.

- Recite the following poem and do the actions:

I can walk on my feet,
Walk, walk, walk.
I can hop on my feet,
Hop, hop, hop.
I can jump with my feet,
Jump, jump, jump.
Now sit down and rest.

I can march with my feet,
March, march, march.
I can tiptoe on my feet,
Tiptoe, tiptoe.
I can run with my feet,
Run, run, run.
Now sit down and rest.

'Round and Stop

- Two-year-olds love to run and stop. This game gives them an opportunity to develop their motor and listening skills as they run around the room.

- Say "'round and 'round and 'round and stop!" As you say the words, walk around the room, and on the word "stop," sit down on a chair.

- Ask your two-year-old to join you in the game. Hold her hand as you move around, or let her walk alone.

- Once she has the idea, try other movements such as jumping, marching, hopping, and crawling.

- Your child will love the "stop" part!

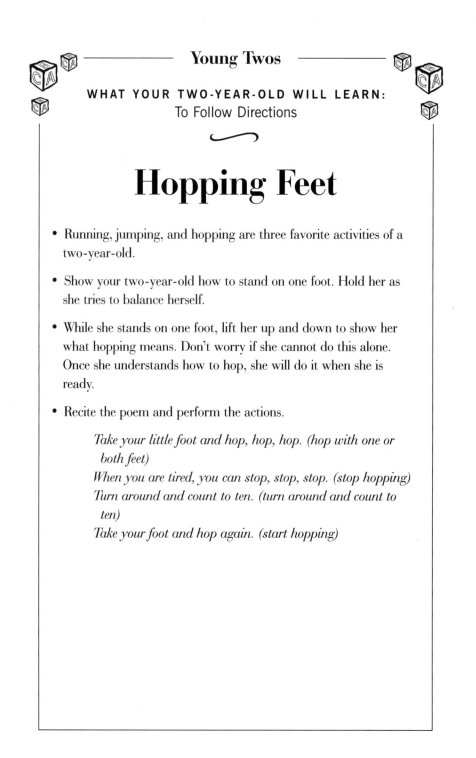

Hopping Feet

- Running, jumping, and hopping are three favorite activities of a two-year-old.

- Show your two-year-old how to stand on one foot. Hold her as she tries to balance herself.

- While she stands on one foot, lift her up and down to show her what hopping means. Don't worry if she cannot do this alone. Once she understands how to hop, she will do it when she is ready.

- Recite the poem and perform the actions.

    Take your little foot and hop, hop, hop. (hop with one or both feet)
    When you are tired, you can stop, stop, stop. (stop hopping)
    Turn around and count to ten. (turn around and count to ten)
    Take your foot and hop again. (start hopping)

The Pilot

- Ask your child to stretch her arms out to the side.

- Show her how to run around the room like an airplane, saying, "Zoom."

- Tell your child, "Now it's time to come in for a landing." Show her how to move more slowly and finally land.

How Many Steps?

- Stand close to a door and say the following rhyme:

  How many steps do I have to take
  To get from here to the door?
  Please count the steps I take
  Walking across the floor
  One…two… (say the
  numbers as you take
  steps)

- Repeat the poem while holding your child's hand as she
  walks with you.

- Experiment with the way that
  you step. Take large steps,
  small steps, hopping steps,
  jumping steps, and so on.

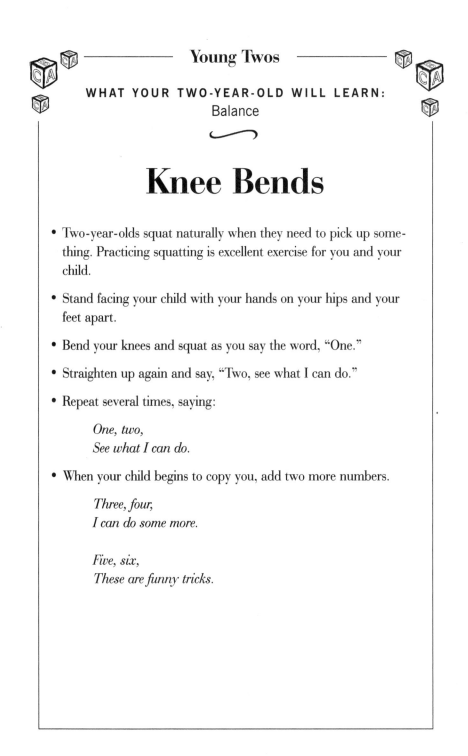

Knee Bends

- Two-year-olds squat naturally when they need to pick up something. Practicing squatting is excellent exercise for you and your child.

- Stand facing your child with your hands on your hips and your feet apart.

- Bend your knees and squat as you say the word, "One."

- Straighten up again and say, "Two, see what I can do."

- Repeat several times, saying:

  One, two,
  See what I can do.

- When your child begins to copy you, add two more numbers.

  Three, four,
  I can do some more.

  Five, six,
  These are funny tricks.

Pointing with Teddy

- Recite the following poem with your child and do the actions:

> *Point to your eye, (point to your own eye)*
> *Point to your nose, (point to your own nose)*
> *Point to your tummy, (point to your own tummy)*
> *And point to your toes. (point to your own toes)*
> *Hello, eye! (blink eyes)*
> *Hello, nose! (wiggle nose)*
> *Hello, tummy! (rub tummy)*
> *Hello, toes! (wiggle toes)*

- Take a teddy bear (or other stuffed animal), and as you say the poem, let the teddy point to those parts of your child's body.

- Encourage your child to help the teddy bear.

Dancing with Bears

- Show your child how to hold a teddy bear (or other stuffed animal) and dance around the room.

- Play different kinds of music for dancing.

- With slow music, glide or take very slow steps.

- With syncopated music, jump, hop, or gallop.

- With fast music, run.

- When the music is finished, put the teddy bear down and say, "Thank you, Teddy, for dancing with me."

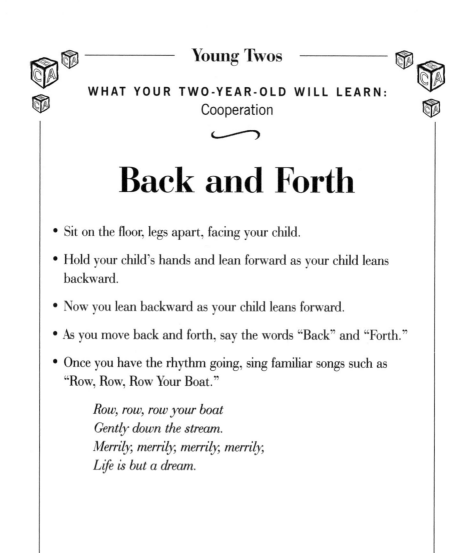

Back and Forth

- Sit on the floor, legs apart, facing your child.

- Hold your child's hands and lean forward as your child leans backward.

- Now you lean backward as your child leans forward.

- As you move back and forth, say the words "Back" and "Forth."

- Once you have the rhythm going, sing familiar songs such as "Row, Row, Row Your Boat."

> *Row, row, row your boat*
> *Gently down the stream.*
> *Merrily, merrily, merrily, merrily,*
> *Life is but a dream.*

Little Boy Blue

- This rhyme helps young children develop good listening skills and practice acting out words they hear.

- Say the following nursery rhyme and act out the words:

  Little Boy Blue, come blow your horn. (pretend to blow a horn, trumpet, clarinet, and so on)
  The sheep's in the meadow, (crawl around on all fours and say, "Baa baa")
  The cow's in the corn. (crawl around on all fours and say, "Moo, moo")
  Where's the little boy who looks after the sheep? (hold your child's hand and look everywhere for Little Boy Blue)
  He's under the haystack fast asleep. (lay down on the floor and close your eyes as if you were sleeping)

Jack Be Nimble

- Say the following nursery rhyme to your two-year-old.

  Jack be nimble,
  Jack be quick,
  Jack jump over
  The candlestick.

- As you say the rhyme, hold your child's hand and, on the word "jump," jump with her.

- Try to stay very still until you say, "Jump." This will not be easy.

- After your child understands the game, place a small object on the floor for her to jump over.

- Begin with a small block. Hold her hand and, on "jump," help her jump over the block.

- Add other objects to jump over as she succeeds with each one.

WHAT YOUR TWO-YEAR-OLD WILL LEARN:
Creativity

Jack and Jill

- Recite the nursery rhyme "Jack and Jill" with your child and act it out.

- Decide who will be Jack and who will be Jill.

> *Jack and Jill went up the hill*
> *To fetch a pail of water. (hold your child's hand and pretend*
> *to walk up a hill)*
> *Jack fell down ("Jack" should fall down)*
> *And broke his crown, (put your hand to your head and say,*
> *"Boo hoo, boo hoo")*
> *And Jill came tumbling after.*
> *("Jill" should fall down and*
> *turn over on the floor)*

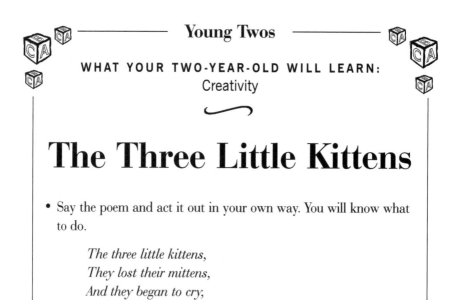

The Three Little Kittens

- Say the poem and act it out in your own way. You will know what to do.

> *The three little kittens,*
> *They lost their mittens,*
> *And they began to cry;*
> *"Oh, mother dear, we sadly fear,*
> *Our mittens we have lost."*
> *"What! Lost your mittens,*
> *You naughty kittens,*
> *You shall have no pie."*
> *Meow, meow, meow.*
>
> *The three little kittens,*
> *They found their mittens,*
> *And they began to cry;*
> *"Oh, mother dear, see here, see here,*
> *Our mittens we have found."*
> *"Found your mittens, you good little kittens,*
> *Now you may have some pie."*
> *Meow, meow, meow.*

AUTHOR'S NOTE: I remember loving this poem as a child. My children loved it, and I'm sure your children will feel the same.

Seesaw, Margery Daw

- Sit on the floor facing your two-year-old.

- Hold her hands and rock back and forth as you say the following nursery rhyme:

  Seesaw, Margery Daw,
  Jacky shall have a new master.
  Jacky shall have but a penny a day,
  Because he can work no faster.

- Start slowly and then go faster and faster.

- There are other ways to rock. You can hold your child in your arms and rock her back and forth, or you can stand facing one another and rock while on your feet.

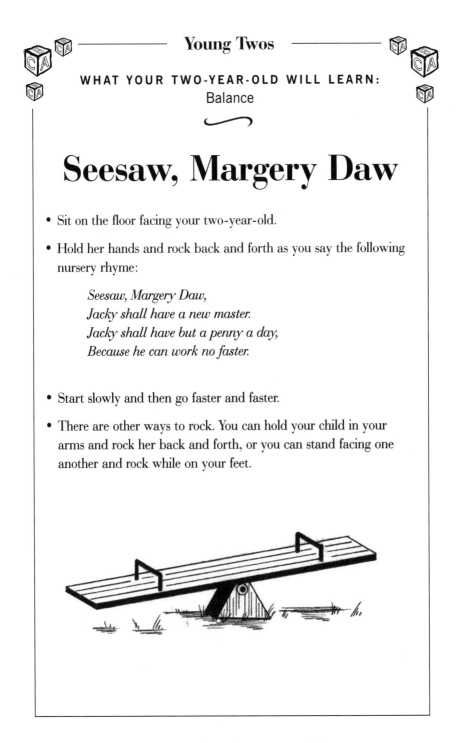

Making a Trail

- Go for a walk with your child. As you go along, tie crepe paper streamers on landmarks—a tree, a lamppost, or a fence.

- Ask your child to help you tie the streamers so that she will better remember where they are.

- After you have gone about two blocks, tell your child, "Now we are going back, and the streamers will help us find our way."

- As you return, untie the streamers.

- Count the streamers as you tie them and as you untie them.

- If you walk along a beach, or play the game in the snow, you can use footprints to find your way back.

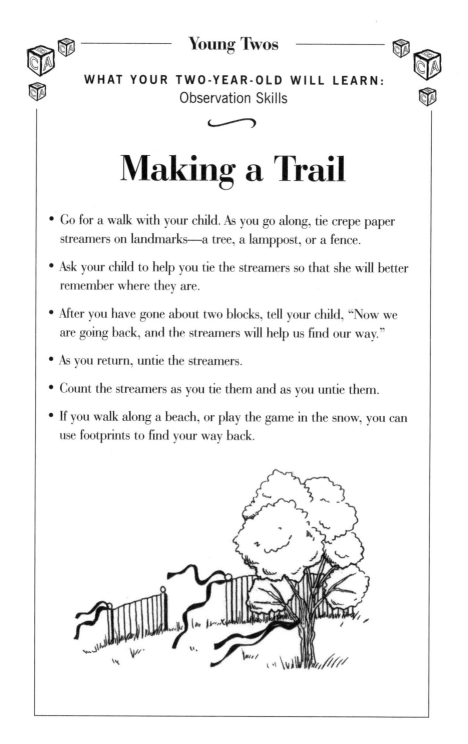

Ring Around the Rosy

- Hold your child's hand as you walk with her in a circle.

- Sing the song "Ring Around the Rosy," and on the words "Ashes, ashes, we all fall down," fall to the ground while holding your child's hand.

  Ring around the rosy,
  A pocketful of posies,
  Ashes, ashes,
  We all fall down.

- While on the ground, sing the following words to the same melody:

  Ring around the rosy,
  A pocketful of posies,
  Daisies, daisies,
  We all get up.

- On the words "We all get up," stand up while holding your child's hands.

- Your two-year-old will want to play this game over and over.

This Is the Way

- Sing these verses to the tune of "Here We Go 'Round the Mulberry Bush." Do the actions as you sing the words.

  This is the way we clap our hands,
  Clap our hands, clap our hands.
  This is the way we clap our hands,
  So early in the morning.

- You can substitute many other actions.

  This is the way we jump up and down...
  This is the way we swing our arms...
  This is the way we stamp our feet...
  This is the way we click our tongues...
  This is the way we throw a kiss...
  This is the way we jump around...

Playing with Scarves

- There are many things to do with scarves and two-year-olds love doing all of them.

- Play music and let your child move to the music with a scarf. Model for her the ways that you can swoop the scarf over your head, behind your back, in and out, and down low to the ground.

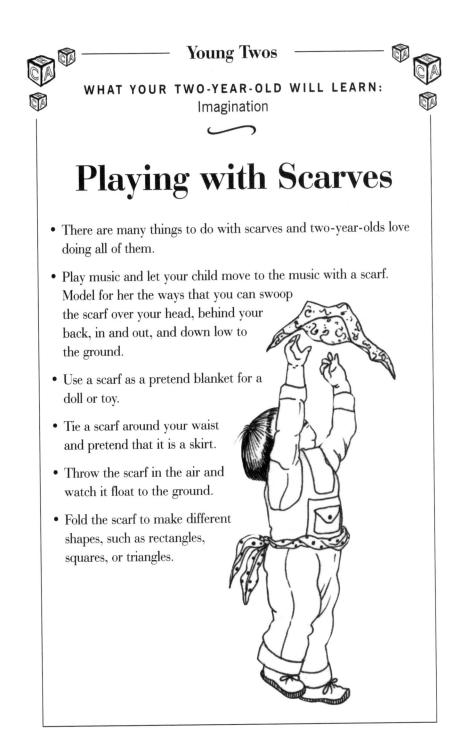

- Use a scarf as a pretend blanket for a doll or toy.

- Tie a scarf around your waist and pretend that it is a skirt.

- Throw the scarf in the air and watch it float to the ground.

- Fold the scarf to make different shapes, such as rectangles, squares, or triangles.

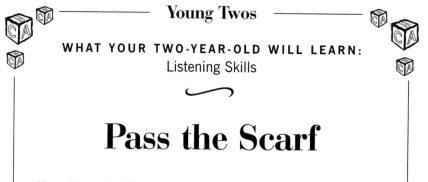

Pass the Scarf

- You will need a CD player or tape player for this game.

- Select some instrumental music that is happy and bright.

- Show your child how to dance around while moving a scarf.

- Explain to your child that you are going to pass the scarf back and forth to one another until the music stops. When the music stops, whoever has the scarf will dance with it.

- Little ones love this game and can't wait to get the scarf.

- If your child has to dance without waiting for the music to stop, that's okay too.

WHAT YOUR TWO-YEAR-OLD WILL LEARN:
Language Skills

Jack-in-the-Box

- Fingerplays are wonderful ways to practice language and use both sides of the brain.

- Say the following rhyme and do the actions.

> *Jack-in-the-box, (make a fist by putting your thumb inside*
> *your fingers)*
> *Sit so still.*
> *Why don't you come out?*
> *I think I will. (pull your thumb out from under your fingers*
> *and make a popping sound with your*
> *mouth)*

WHAT YOUR TWO-YEAR-OLD WILL LEARN:
Fun

Rain on the Green Grass

- This rhyme can be a wonderful catalyst for language development. Say the following to your child:

    Rain on the green grass,
    Rain on the sea,
    Rain on the housetops,
    But not on me!

- When you come to the words "But not on me," put your hands on your hips and shake your head "no" vigorously.

- Substitute familiar words for the words in the poem. For example:

    Rain on the table,
    Rain on the floor,
    Rain on the doggie,
    But not on me!

- Soon your child will get the idea and will tell you what words to say. Always end with the same words, "But not on me!"

Five Little Fingers

- Ask your two-year-old to hold up her hand. Tell her she has five fingers.

- Hold up your hand and wiggle each finger as you count up to five.

- Chant the following:

  What can I do with five little fingers?
  What can I do with five little fingers?
  What can I do with five little fingers?
  What can I do today?

- As you say it, wiggle your fingers in the air

  I can shake my five little fingers,
  I can shake my five little fingers,
  I can shake my five little fingers,
  I can shake them today.

- Here are other things to do with five little fingers.

  I can wiggle my five little fingers....
  I can wave my five little fingers....
  I can pat with five little fingers....
  I can turn the wheel with five little fingers....
  I can beep the horn with five little fingers....

Touch Your Nose

- This is a nice fingerplay for a quiet time.

- Ask your child to touch her nose, her chin, her eyes, her knees, her hair, her ears, and her elbows.

- Say the following poem and act it out.

> *Touch your nose,*
> *Touch your chin,*
> *That is how the game begins.*
> *Touch your eyes,*
> *Touch your knees,*
> *Now pretend you're going to sneeze.*
> *Touch your hair,*
> *Touch your ears,*
> *Touch your sweet lips right here.*
> *Touch your elbows,*
> *Make them bend,*
> *Now this little game will end.*

The Cobbler

- Shoes and feet are fascinating to two-year-olds. They enjoy taking their shoes off and on.

- Play a cobbler game with your child.

- Tell her that you are a cobbler who is going to fix her shoe. Hold the shoe in your hand and say, "Bang and a bang and a bang, bang, bang."

- As you say these words, pretend to hammer on the shoe.

- Then say, "All fixed! You can wear it now."

- Ask your child to fix your shoe. As she hammers, say the same words, "Bang and a bang and a bang, bang, bang."

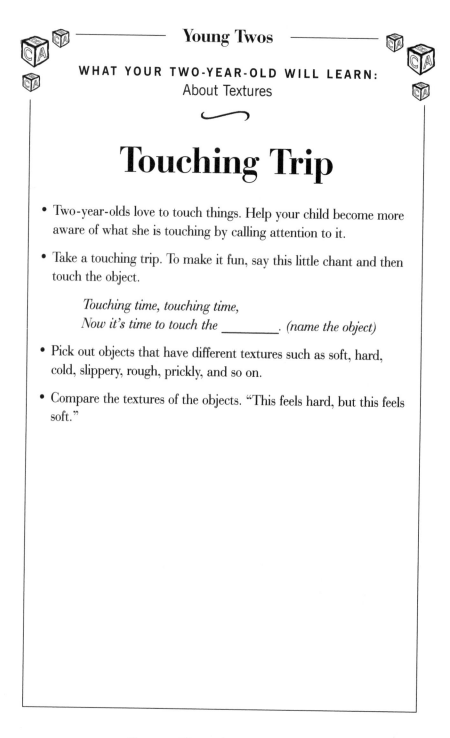

WHAT YOUR TWO-YEAR-OLD WILL LEARN:
About Textures

Touching Trip

- Two-year-olds love to touch things. Help your child become more aware of what she is touching by calling attention to it.

- Take a touching trip. To make it fun, say this little chant and then touch the object.

  Touching time, touching time,
  Now it's time to touch the _____. (name the object)

- Pick out objects that have different textures such as soft, hard, cold, slippery, rough, prickly, and so on.

- Compare the textures of the objects. "This feels hard, but this feels soft."

Inside Snow

- Why not bring snow inside, and let your two-year-old play with it?

- Here are things that you can do with snow.
  - Spoon it into a dish.
  - Color it with food coloring.
  - Watch it melt.
  - Make little snowballs.
  - Make a miniature snowman and put it in the freezer.

A Sound Walk

- Two-year-old children are inquisitive about the world around them. This game develops their awareness of the environment.

- Walk outside with your child and listen for sounds around you, such as:
  - Wind blowing
  - Birds chirping
  - Leaves rustling
  - Cars driving
  - Dogs barking
  - People talking

- Talk about the sounds with your child, and see if you can imitate them.

Where Do You Think the Birdie Lives?

- When you are outdoors, observe the birds and talk about where they live, the sounds that they make, and their color.

- Here is a fingerplay about birds to do with your child.

- Hold your child's palm facing you. As you say the rhyme, take your hand and move it around and around her palm. When you come to the words "Up into his house," slowly crawl your fingers up your child's arm, and on the word "house," tickle her under the chin.

> *Where do you think the birdie lives?*
> *Where do you think the birdie lives?*
> *'Round and 'round and*
> *'Round and 'round and*
> *Up into his house.*

- Switch parts and let your child play the game on your hand.

The Clock Game

- Tell your child that clocks go, "Tick, tock." Tell her that you will pretend to be a clock.

- Tell your child that the clock is going to hide and she is going to try to find it.

- Walk around the room stiffly with your arms to your sides, saying, "Tick, tock, tick, tock."

- It is okay if your child watches where you hide.

- Now say, "Can you find the clock? Tick, tock, tick, tock."

- When your child finds you, say, "You found the clock!"

- After you have played this game for awhile, your child will want to be the clock.

Listening Game

- Pick three objects that are familiar to your two-year-old, for example, a whistle, a rattle, a toy that makes noise, or an alarm clock.

- Talk about each object and the sound that it makes.

- Show your child one of the objects. Ask her to close her eyes and listen to the sound.

- Put the object down. Ask her to open her eyes and give you the thing that was making the noise.

- Repeat this with each article until you are sure that your two-year-old knows what each one sounds like.

What's Inside?

- Gather three or four plastic containers with lids. Margarine tubs work very well. Put a solid object, such as a small block, a plastic spoon, or a piece of fabric, inside each tub.

- Shake one of the containers and describe the sound to your child. Use words such as "loud," "soft," or "jingly."

- Repeat this activity with another container.

- Ask your child to give you the container that makes the "soft sound."

- Ask your child to take off the lid and see what is inside.

- After all of the containers have been explored and discussed, let your child put the objects into the containers and put the lids on again.

The Piano Game

- You don't have to know how to play a piano in order to explore one with your two-year-old.

- Look at the piano keys and talk about the colors. Play a black key, and then play a white key. Name the color as you play it.

- Play the keys on the upper right to make tiny raindrop sounds.

- Play the keys on the lower left to make thunder sounds.

- Make up a story about the little raindrops that fell from the sky. Play the upper right keys and keep going down to the lower left keys.

- Make up a song at the piano. Pick any two keys. Play them in a variety of ways such as repeating, alternating, softly, loudly, with a pedal, and so on. Make up questions and answers. For example, play the first note and say, "How are you today?" Play the second note and say, "I am fine today."

- Encourage your child to play music on the piano. If you do not have a piano, use other musical instruments, such as a bell or a drum.

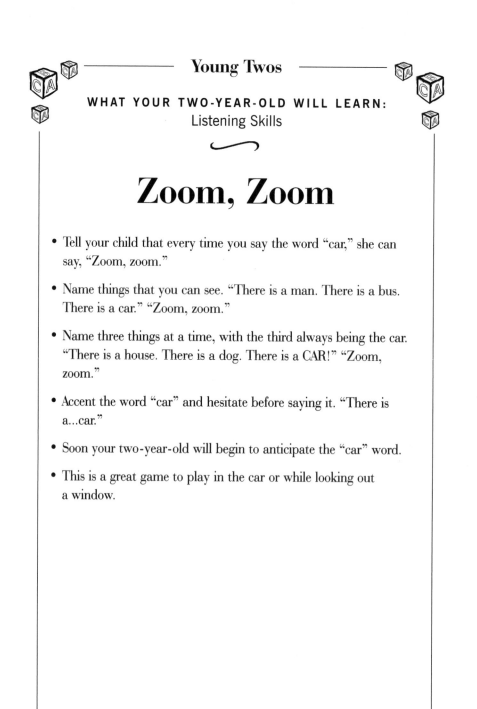

WHAT YOUR TWO-YEAR-OLD WILL LEARN:
Listening Skills

Zoom, Zoom

- Tell your child that every time you say the word "car," she can say, "Zoom, zoom."

- Name things that you can see. "There is a man. There is a bus. There is a car." "Zoom, zoom."

- Name three things at a time, with the third always being the car. "There is a house. There is a dog. There is a CAR!" "Zoom, zoom."

- Accent the word "car" and hesitate before saying it. "There is a...car."

- Soon your two-year-old will begin to anticipate the "car" word.

- This is a great game to play in the car or while looking out a window.

Look What I See!

- Put two chairs in front of a window.

- Begin a conversation about what you see through the window. Ask, "What do you see in the yard?"

- Whatever the answer is, respond to it with a related question. For example, if your child says, "Car," then ask, "Where is the car going?"

- Encourage your child to talk.

- Later in the day find magazines with pictures of what you saw through the window.

- Show the pictures to your child and remind her of what you talked about earlier.

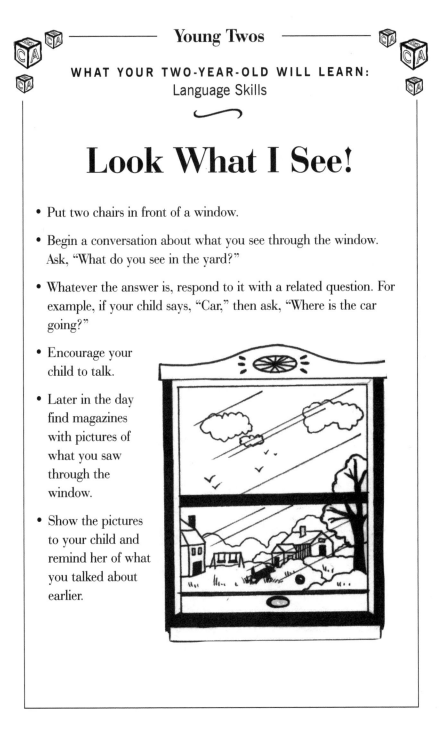

WHAT YOUR TWO-YEAR-OLD WILL LEARN:
Listening Skills

Sing the Word

- This is a great game to develop your child's listening skills.

- Sing the first line of a favorite song such as, "Mary Had a Little Lamb." Ask your child to sing it with you.

- Sing it again very softly until you come to the word "lamb." Sing that word in a louder voice.

- Sing it again, omitting the word "lamb" and encouraging your two-year-old to say the missing word.

- When your child understands how the game is played, try the second line.

- Soon you will be able to sing the entire song, leaving out the last word in each line for your two-year-old to say.

Oh, Hush-a-Bye My Darling

- Language games are fun to play in the car. Try chanting the following:

  Riding in the car, car,
  Riding in the car, car,
  Riding in the car, car,
  Oh, hush-a-bye, my darling.

- This time change the word "darling" to another affectionate term such as "sweetie" or "honey."

  Riding in the car, car,
  Riding in the car, car,
  Riding in the car, car,
  Oh, hush-a-bye, my honey.

- Think of all the different words that you can substitute for the last word.

  AUTHOR'S NOTE: I was experimenting with this poem, and one child said, "Oh, piece of pie, my darling." She thought it was pretty funny, so we changed the last line.

The Three Bears

- Tell your two-year-old the story of the three bears. Emphasize big, middle-sized, and small.

- The story should be a shortened version. Use different voices for each character.

- Each time you say, "Somebody's been eating my porridge," encourage your child to say the words with you.

- Get three teddy bears and tell the story again, using the bears as puppets saying each character's words.

- This is a wonderful language experience for young children.

Games to Play with Two-Year-Olds

Listen to My Name

- Two-year-olds enjoy simple rhymes and songs.

- Substitute your child's name in familiar rhymes and songs.

    Old (child's name) had a farm...
    Eensy Weensy (child's name) went up the water spout...
    Little boy (child's name) come blow your horn...
    Diddle, diddle, dumpling, my son (child's name)...

- Once your child enjoys this game, try substituting other names such as grandma, sister, mom, and other people who are familiar to your child.

Greeting Song

- Sing this "Good Morning" song each morning to the tune of "Are You Sleeping?"

    Are you sleeping, are you sleeping
    Little _____ (child's name), little _____ (child's name)?
    Now it's time to wake up.
    Now it's time to wake up.
    I like you; I like you.

- Change the first line to help your child learn about parts of her body. For example:

    Where's your nose, where's your nose?

- You can also ask questions with this song.

    Are you hungry, are you hungry?

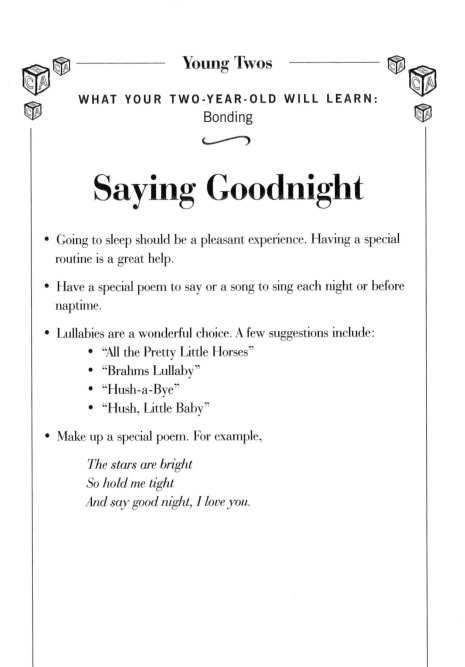

Saying Goodnight

- Going to sleep should be a pleasant experience. Having a special routine is a great help.

- Have a special poem to say or a song to sing each night or before naptime.

- Lullabies are a wonderful choice. A few suggestions include:
    - "All the Pretty Little Horses"
    - "Brahms Lullaby"
    - "Hush-a-Bye"
    - "Hush, Little Baby"

- Make up a special poem. For example,

    The stars are bright
    So hold me tight
    And say good night, I love you.

Family Talk

- Gather pictures of family members.

- Show the pictures to your child and identify each picture with a single name, such as "Mommy," "Daddy," "Papa," "Nanny," and so on.

- Spread the pictures out on a table, and ask your child to find a specific person.

- Hold up a picture and say to your two-year-old, "Who is this?" Whatever her answer may be, repeat the correct answer.

- Look at the pictures again and say something about each person after they have been identified. For example: "Papa loves you very much" or "Nanny has a pretty smile."

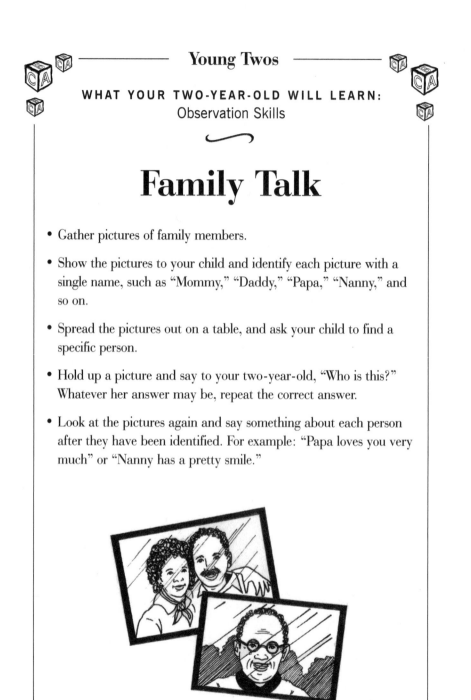

Building a Train

- Collect two groups of blocks, one for you and one for your child.

- Invite your child to make a train with you. Put down one of your blocks and ask her to put down one of hers. (Encourage her to choose a matching block from her group.)

- Continue placing blocks next to one another.

- Talk about the train you are making together. Touch one block and say, "This is the block that you put down." Point to another block and say, "This is the block that I put down."

- Play a train game with your child. Move the train of blocks and say, "Here comes the train. Choo, choo, choo."

- When children have an opportunity to play both roles, the leader and the follower, they begin to understand what working together means.

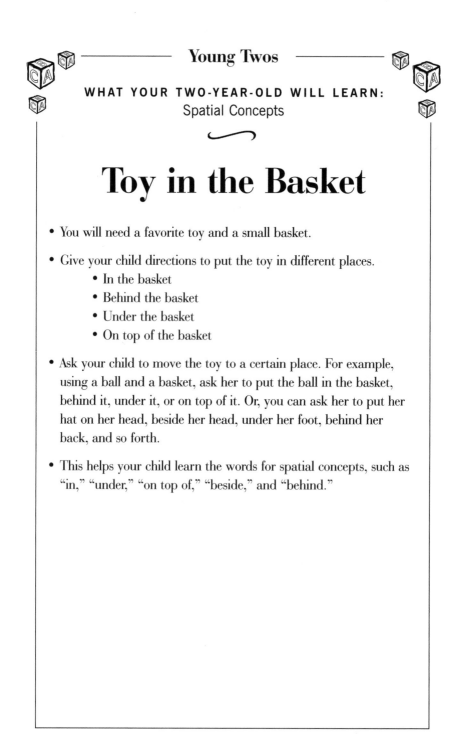

Toy in the Basket

- You will need a favorite toy and a small basket.

- Give your child directions to put the toy in different places.
  - In the basket
  - Behind the basket
  - Under the basket
  - On top of the basket

- Ask your child to move the toy to a certain place. For example, using a ball and a basket, ask her to put the ball in the basket, behind it, under it, or on top of it. Or, you can ask her to put her hat on her head, beside her head, under her foot, behind her back, and so forth.

- This helps your child learn the words for spatial concepts, such as "in," "under," "on top of," "beside," and "behind."

Washing Fun

- Not all two-year-olds like to take baths, but almost all two-year-olds like to "give" baths.

- Select a doll that is washable and ask your child to bathe the doll.

- Make suggestions about washing certain parts of the doll's body. "Can you wash the doll's legs? Toes? Neck?"

- When the doll's bath is over, let your child dry the doll and put it to bed.

- Your child also may enjoy washing plastic dishes.

Games to Play with Two-Year-Olds

Water Games

- There is something very satisfying about playing with water, and
  two-year-olds have a great attraction to water. Here are some
  water games that they will enjoy.
    - Wiping tabletops and countertops with a sponge.
    - Spraying water with a spray bottle on objects and wiping
      them dry.
    - Washing dishes and putting them into another container
      for rinsing.
    - Pouring water from one container to another. (This is a
      great bathtub game.)
    - Filling a baster with water and squishing it out.
    - Floating water toys in the bathtub.
    - Experimenting with what sinks or floats in a bathtub.

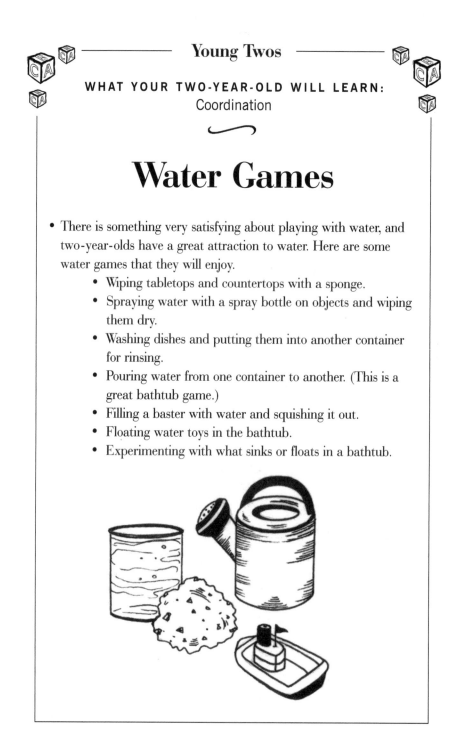

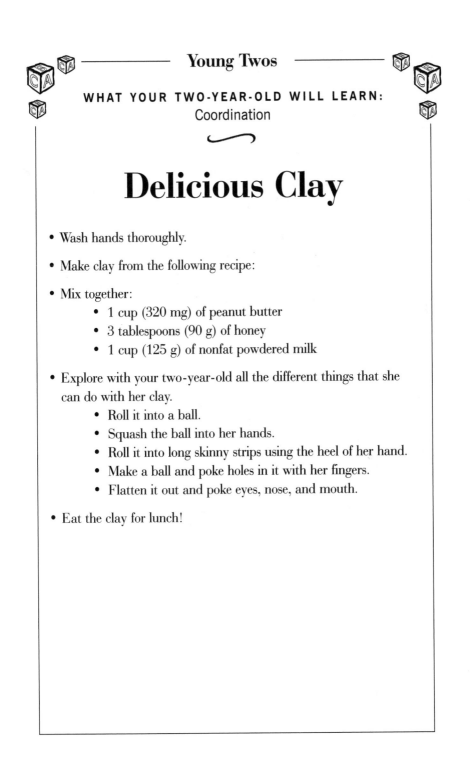

Delicious Clay

- Wash hands thoroughly.

- Make clay from the following recipe:

- Mix together:
    - 1 cup (320 mg) of peanut butter
    - 3 tablespoons (90 g) of honey
    - 1 cup (125 g) of nonfat powdered milk

- Explore with your two-year-old all the different things that she can do with her clay.
    - Roll it into a ball.
    - Squash the ball into her hands.
    - Roll it into long skinny strips using the heel of her hand.
    - Make a ball and poke holes in it with her fingers.
    - Flatten it out and poke eyes, nose, and mouth.

- Eat the clay for lunch!

Shape Collage

- Choose one shape such as a circle, square, triangle, or heart that you would like your two-year-old to learn about.

- Cut that shape out of a variety of materials, including paper, foil, fabric, and any others that are safe and appropriate.

- Use a large piece of construction paper for the base.

- Put a dab of glue on the back of one shape, and show your child how to glue it onto the construction paper.

- Give your two-year-old the same shape cut from another material. Put some glue on it and let her put it down on the paper.

- Talk about the shapes as she builds her collage.

- Continue to give her one shape at a time until they are all used.

- Compliment your child on creating the collage.

- Hang the collage in a spot where your child can see it.

WHAT YOUR TWO-YEAR-OLD WILL LEARN:
About Textures

Rubbing with Crayons

- Gather objects with interesting textures such as leaves, wood, rocks, or large buttons.

- Remove the paper wrappings from several crayons.

- Place a piece of paper over one of the objects, and encourage your child to rub a crayon over the paper.

- Your child will be delighted with the results. It's almost like magic!

- Go outside and experiment with rubbings over tree bark, cement, and anything else that you think would be interesting.

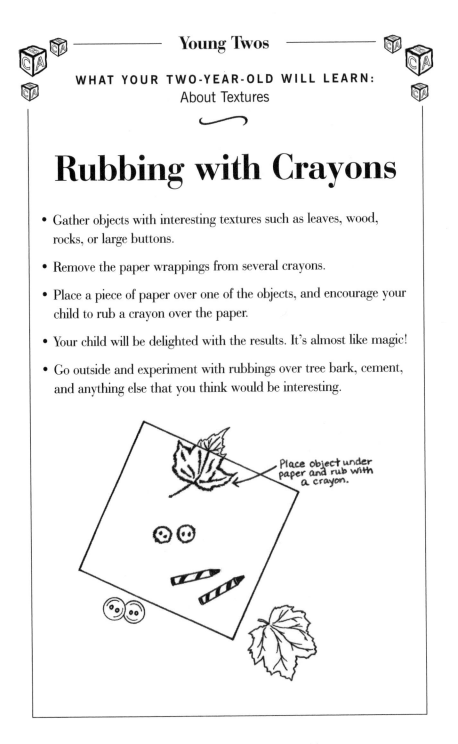

Place object under paper and rub with a crayon.

Paper Fun

- Tearing paper is a wonderful game to strengthen fine motor skills.

- Give your child pieces of paper from magazines, catalogs, and newspapers.

- Suggest different ways to tear the paper—in little pieces, big pieces, long pieces, and short pieces.

- Take the torn pieces of paper and make a collage.

- Use papers with different textures. Tissue paper, wrapping paper, wax paper, and paper towels are interesting for children to experiment with. Some paper will tear more easily than others.

- Tear the paper into very small pieces, throw them into the air, and pretend that it is snowing.

Pizza Fun

- Buy a ready-made pizza crust.

- Go to a local salad bar and pick out a variety of sliced vegetables and cheeses to decorate your pizza, such as green and red peppers, olives, shredded cheese, carrot strips, celery strips, pineapple chunks, or raisins.

- Show your child how to sprinkle cheese on top of the pizza crust.

- Put out all of the salad ingredients, and encourage your child to decorate the pizza any way that she wants. If you desire, add sauce before the toppings.

- Put it in the oven, bake, and enjoy.

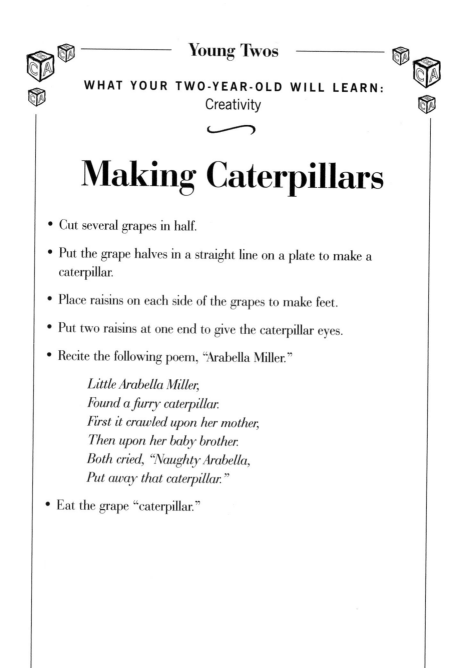

Making Caterpillars

- Cut several grapes in half.

- Put the grape halves in a straight line on a plate to make a caterpillar.

- Place raisins on each side of the grapes to make feet.

- Put two raisins at one end to give the caterpillar eyes.

- Recite the following poem, "Arabella Miller."

> *Little Arabella Miller,*
> *Found a furry caterpillar.*
> *First it crawled upon her mother,*
> *Then upon her baby brother.*
> *Both cried, "Naughty Arabella,*
> *Put away that caterpillar."*

- Eat the grape "caterpillar."

WHAT YOUR TWO-YEAR-OLD WILL LEARN:
Body Awareness

Body Food

- Talk with your two-year-old about the parts of her face. Questions such as "Where is your nose?" and "Where are your eyes?" will delight your child.

- Draw a large circle on a piece of paper and draw the parts of the face that you talked about with your child.

- Slice an orange so it makes circles. Using raisins for eyes, nuts for the nose, and a pimento for the mouth, show your two-year-old how to make a face on the orange slice. Eat this yummy face!

- Cut several more slices and let your child make faces by herself.

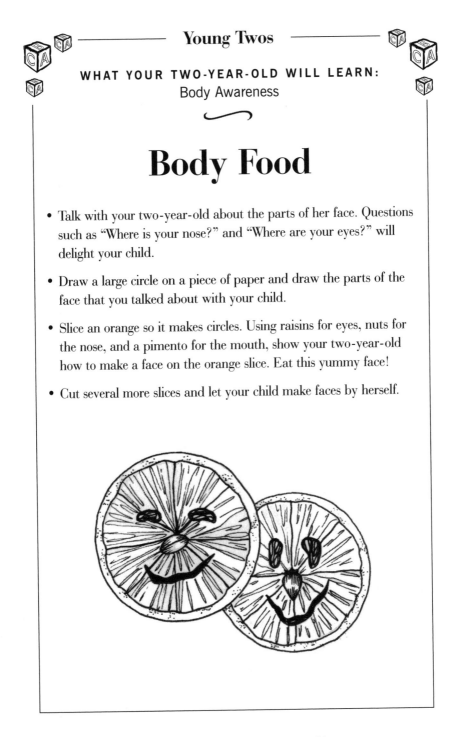

Berry Nice

- Berries have interesting flavors and textures and they are nutritious, as well.

- Select two kinds of berries with different colors and textures, for example, blueberries and strawberries.

- Show your child how to wash the berries and pat them dry.

- Sort them into two piles, naming them as you sort.

- Let your child taste the berries.

- Pour vanilla yogurt into a dish.

- Ask your two-year-old to add the berries to the yogurt.

- Eat and enjoy.

Banana Treats

- Tell your child a story about a monkey whose name was _____ (child's name), who swung from tree to tree looking for bananas.

- Pretend to swing from a tree and make monkey sounds. Pretend to find a banana and peel it.

- Give your two-year-old a banana to peel. She may need help.

- Using a plastic knife, help your child slice the banana.

- Encourage your child to roll the banana slices in cinnamon and nuts; mix the banana with cereal, raisins, or yogurt; or make a banana milk shake by mixing it with milk or yogurt in a blender.

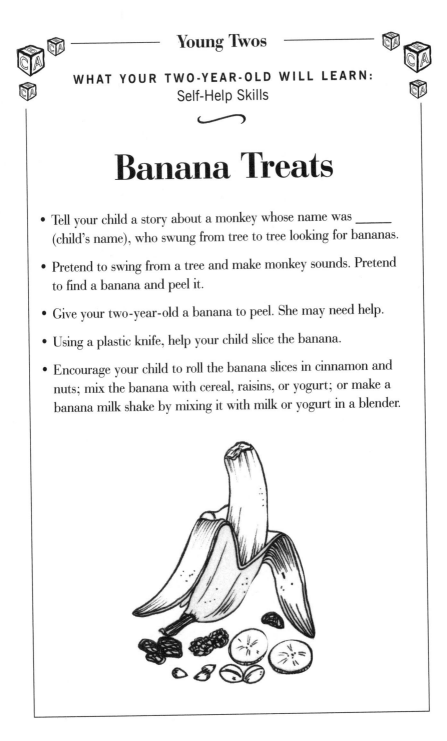

Do-It-Yourself Cereal

- Two-year-olds are becoming more independent and want to do things for themselves.

- This is the "Me do it!" age, and whenever you can provide this opportunity, it will help your child feel good about herself.

- Measure out various ingredients for cereal so your two-year-old can pour them into a bowl and stir them.

- Place three or four ingredients into small bowls, for example, dry cereal, raisins, and wheat germ.

- Give your child a larger bowl and ask her to pour the contents of each of the smaller bowls into it.

- Add milk, stir, and eat!

Sweet Potato Games

- Show your child a sweet potato. Let her feel it, smell it, and roll it in her hands.

- Cook the sweet potato and let her taste it. Microwaving is the fastest way to cook the potato.

- Try growing a sweet potato plant. Stick three or four toothpicks into the sides of the sweet potato so that it will balance in a glass.

- Put the sweet potato in a glass and cover the bottom part with water. Check the potato each day to be sure there is enough water.

- When the sprouts appear, your two-year-old will be delighted.

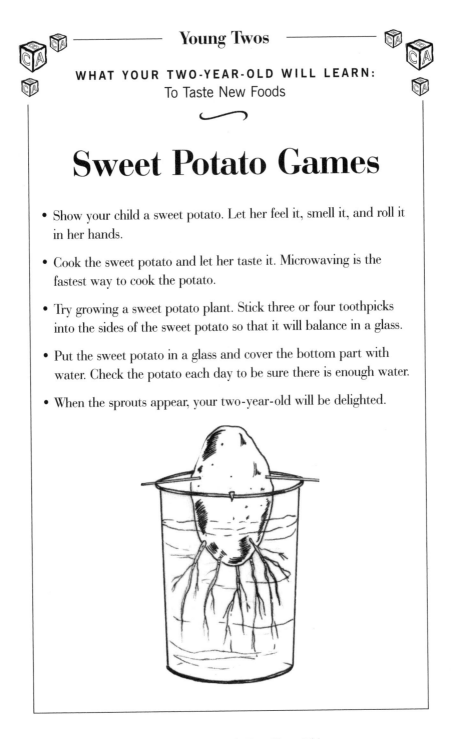

Games to Play with Two-Year-Olds

Sorting Crackers

- Put an assortment of crackers on a placemat. Select interesting shapes and sizes.

- Prepare a placemat for your child and one for yourself.

- Pick up a cracker and talk about its shape, size, and smell.

- Ask your child to find a matching cracker on her placemat. Praise her when she finds the cracker that matches yours.

- After you have matched all the crackers, mix them up and play again.

- Set out cream cheese, softened margarine, or peanut butter and plastic knives. Your child can put one of these spreads on the crackers.

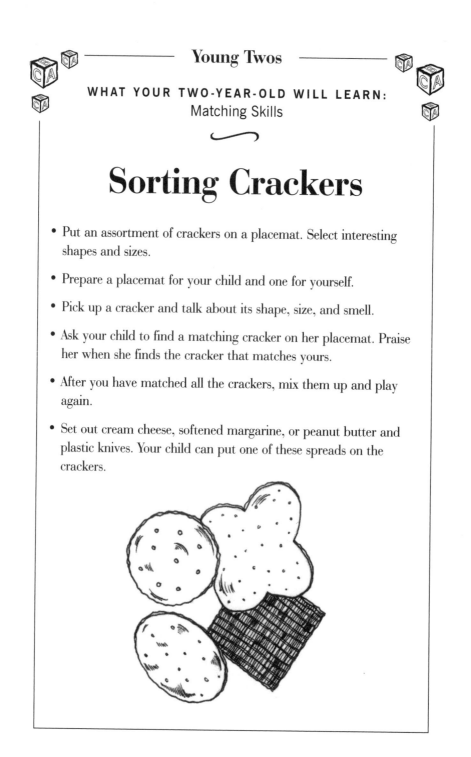

Apple Fun

- Two-year-olds are beginning to identify colors.

- Fill a sack with both red and green apples (no more than six to eight).

- Ask your child to take the apples out of the sack one at a time.

- Each time she takes an apple out of the sack, say, "Oh, boy, a green apple," or "Oh, boy, a red apple."

- When all the apples are out of the sack, sort them into two piles by color.

- Ask your child to put all the red ones back into the sack and then to put all of the green ones back into the sack.

- After you have played this game a few times, your child will begin to understand how to separate the apples by color.

Sponges

- Cooking is fun to do with two-year-olds. Cleaning up the mess can be fun, too.

- Put out two bowls. Fill one with water and leave the other one empty. Show your child how to dip a sponge into the water-filled bowl and squeeze it out into the empty one.

- Your child will love doing this and may stay with this activity for a long time.

- If you see that she is getting bored, show her how to squeeze out the sponge and wipe things. Give her specific items to wipe. "Please wipe the tabletop." "Please wipe the sink."

- By learning how to squeeze first, she will understand that in order to wipe something, she must first squeeze out the water.

One, Two, Boo Hoo Hoo

- Young two-year-olds are beginning to learn a sense of numbers. The more counting experiences they have, the sooner they will acquire the concepts.

- Hold up two fingers and say:

    One, two,
    Boo hoo hoo.

- As you say the words, point to each finger.

- Repeat the same poem, pointing to other parts of the body (of which there are two), such as ears, eyes, knees, elbows, and feet.

- Once your child can play this game, look for other groups of twos inside and outside, or even patterns in clothes or on wallpaper.

- Give your child two blocks. Ask her to pick up the blocks, one at a time, saying the poem.

- Ask her to say the poem while putting the blocks down, one at a time.

Counting Walk

- Take a walk through your house holding your two-year-old's hand.

- Start counting familiar objects, such as chairs. Walk from room to room, saying out loud, "One chair, two chairs," and so on.

- When you reach the number five, stop.

- On a large piece of paper, draw five chairs for your child to see. Count them again.

- Ask your child, "What would you like to count next?"

- Your child will enjoy this game very much.

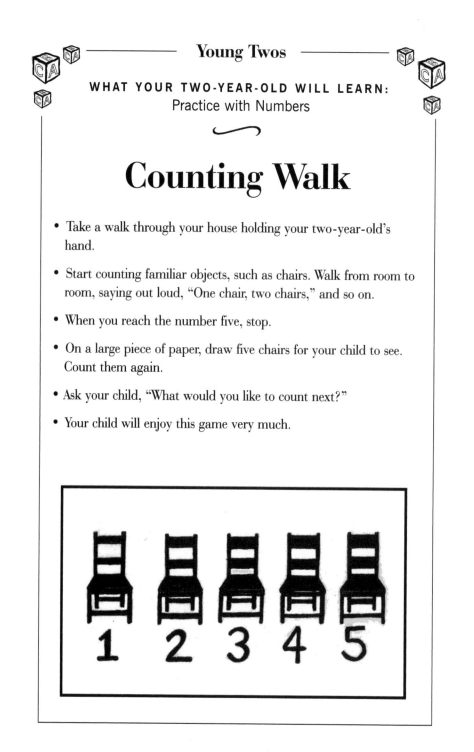

Bell Horses

- This is a lovely old English nursery rhyme to teach your child.

- Say the rhyme while holding your child's hand. Gently hold up one of her fingers on "one o'clock," hold up a second finger on "two o'clock" and so on.

  Bell horses, bell horses,
  What's the time of day?
  One o'clock, two o'clock,
  Time to go away.

  Good horses, bad horses,
  What's the time of day?
  Three o'clock, four o'clock,
  Time to go away.

- This game not only reinforces counting, but familiarizes your child with the names of numbers.

- Show your child how to make a "clip-clop" sound with her tongue.

Me and You

- Recite the following poem with your two-year-old, touching the parts of the body as you name them:

    I've got one head,
    One nose, too.
    One mouth, one chin,
    And so have you.

    I've got two eyes,
    Two ears, too.
    Two arms, two legs,
    And so have you.

    I've got two hands,
    Two thumbs, too.
    I'll wiggle my thumbs,
    And so can you.

- This is fun to do standing in front of a mirror. Your child can see her head, nose, mouth, and other parts of the body as you touch them.

- Recite the poem again, holding your child's hand and helping her identify the parts of the body.

There Were Three

- Recite the following poem. Each time you say the word "three," hold up three fingers.

> *There were three furry cats*
> *Purring by the fire.*
> *Meow, meow, meow,*
> *Purring by the fire.*
>
> *Count with me*
> *Three furry cats.*
> *Count with me,*
> *One, two, three.*
>
> *There were three yellow ducks*
> *Quacking by the road.*
> *Quack, quack, quack,*
> *Quacking by the road.*
>
> *Count with me*
> *Three yellow ducks.*
> *Count with me,*
> *One, two, three.*

- Other ideas include three big cows mooing in the yard, three little pigs playing in the mud, and three little hens sitting on some eggs.

Four Little Puppies

- Talk about puppies with your two-year-old. Look at picture books and imitate the sound that puppies make.

- Recite the poem and do the actions.

> *Four little puppies scratched at the door, (hold up four fingers and move them up and down)*
> *One, two, three, four. (touch each finger)*
> *I gave them some food,*
> *And they trotted out the door. (make your fingers walk away)*

Games to Play with Two-Year-Olds

The Surprise Bag

- Fill a shopping bag with three or four familiar objects.

- Sit on the floor with your two-year-old facing you.

- Very dramatically and very slowly, pull one object out of the shopping bag.

- As you take out the object, ask your child, "Do you know what I am taking out of the bag?"

- Give the object to her to hold as you talk about its name, its color, how it feels, and what it is used for.

- Ask your child to put the object back into the bag.

- Repeat this activity with another object.

- To add a language component to this game, chant the following before taking each object out of the bag.

    Mickety, mackety, mockety mag,
    What do I have inside of my bag?

- Suggestions of objects to put in the bag include a crayon, a toy car, a stuffed animal, a drinking cup, a block, or a ball.

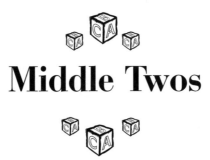

Middle Twos

My Toes Are Starting to Wiggle

- Take off your shoes and your two-year-old's shoes.

- Show him how to wiggle his toes.

- Wiggle your toes while you sing one of your favorite songs.

- Pick additional parts of the body and sing about them as you wiggle them. Elbows, knees, fingers, nose, and ears are fun to do.

- Try wiggling two parts of the body at once.

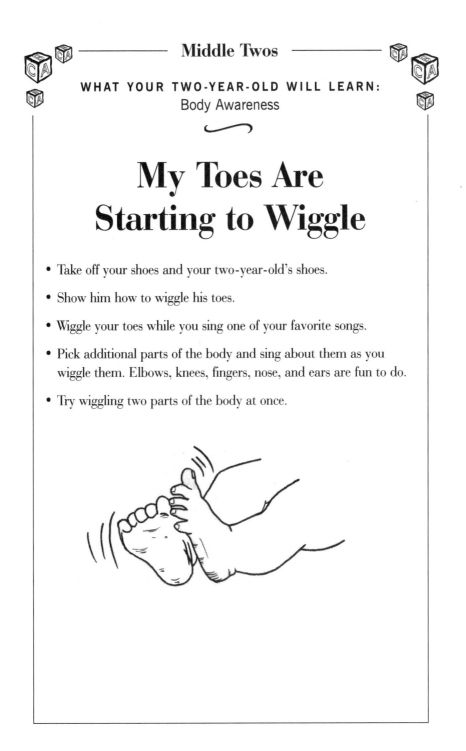

My Hands

- Draw outlines of your hand and your child's hand on a piece of heavy white paper.

- Point out to your child that your hand is larger than his hand.

- Ask your child to color the hands, using large crayons.

- Cut out the shapes and glue them onto a larger piece of paper for hanging on the wall.

- Talk about all the different things that you can do with your hands.

- Ask your child to do many things with his hands.
    - Shake hands.
    - Wave goodbye.
    - Wave hello.
    - Wiggle his fingers.
    - Put his fingers to his lips for "shhh."
    - Hold his hand out for "stop."

WHAT YOUR TWO-YEAR-OLD WILL LEARN:
Imagination

Silly Peek-a-Boo

- Make a silly face. Stick out your tongue, make "fish lips," or scrunch up your face.

- Ask your child to make a silly face. Whatever he does, laugh and encourage him to do more.

- Put your hands over your face and say, "Silly, silly, peek-a-boo." Take your hands away and make a silly face.

- Ask your two-year-old to put his hands over his face. Say again, "Silly, silly, peek-a-boo." Your child will know what to do.

- After you have played this game a few times, make silly sounds to go with your silly face.

Follow the Tape

- Make a path on the floor with masking tape.

- Make the path curve in many different directions.

- Hold your child's hand and walk along the path with him.

- When your two-year-old understands that he can walk on the masking tape and follow it, suggest that you travel the path in a different way.

- Try hopping, running, sliding, marching, walking backward, and tiptoeing.

- Try this game outside.

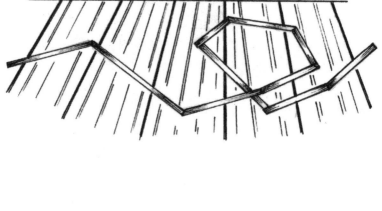

The Movement Game

- Your two-year-old has amazing agility by now and can begin to use the movements he already knows in different ways.

- This game will also increase his vocabulary.

- Demonstrate all the following movements to your child, one at a time, and ask him to imitate you after each demonstration.
  - Take giant steps.
  - Walk backward.
  - Take tiny steps.
  - Walk sideways.
  - Jump fast.
  - March backward.

Across the Room

- Stand on the opposite side of the room facing your child.

- Help your child decide how he will get to the other side of the room where you are. Some ideas are to jump, walk, run, walk backward, walk sideways, hop like a rabbit, or crawl like a cat.

- When he tells you what he is going to do, say, "Ready, set, go!"

- When he reaches you, give him a big hug and say, "Time to go home." He goes back to the other side of the room, and you can play the game again.

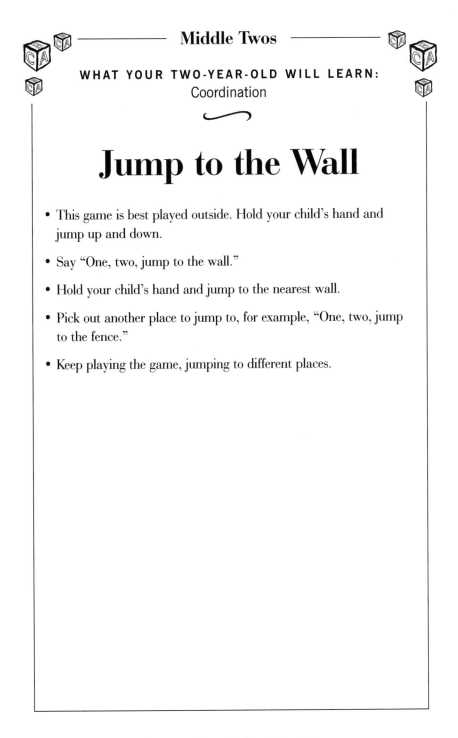

Jump to the Wall

- This game is best played outside. Hold your child's hand and jump up and down.

- Say "One, two, jump to the wall."

- Hold your child's hand and jump to the nearest wall.

- Pick out another place to jump to, for example, "One, two, jump to the fence."

- Keep playing the game, jumping to different places.

Creatures

- Show your two-year-old pictures of a fish, a bird, and a caterpillar.

- Talk about how each of these animals moves. A fish swims, a bird flies, and a caterpillar crawls.

- Pretend you are swimming like a fish.

- Pretend you are flying like a bird.

- Pretend you are crawling like a caterpillar.

- Recite the following rhyme and perform the actions.

  Swim, little fish, in water clear,
  Fly, little bird, up in the air,
  Creep, little caterpillar, creep, creep,
  Sleep, little children, sleep, sleep. (close your eyes and pre-
     tend to be sleeping)

Two Little Blackbirds

- Say the poem and do the actions.

    Two little blackbirds sitting on the hill, (hold up the pointer
    finger of each hand)
    One named Jack and one named Jill. (wiggle "Jack" and
    then wiggle "Jill")
    Fly away, Jack. (wiggle your finger behind your back in a
    flying motion)
    Fly away, Jill. (wiggle your other finger behind your back in
    a flying motion)
    Come back, Jack. (bring Jack back)
    Come back, Jill. (bring Jill back)

- Pretend that you and your child are Jack and Jill. Recite the poem
  and act out the words. For the lines that say "Fly away," find a
  place in the room to hide. On the words "Come back," come out
  from your hiding place.

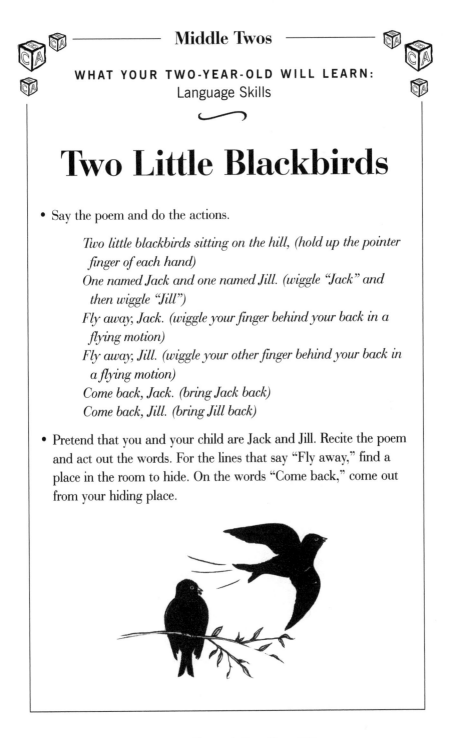

The Sticker Trail

- Young children love stickers!

- Find a place to make a sticker trail on the floor. Make sure you use stickers that won't stick permanently!

- Make a path on the floor that ends behind a chair or sofa.

- Show your child how to follow the path to the very end.

- At the end of the path, have a doll or stuffed animal waiting for a hug.

- Pretend to be a dog "woofing" along the path. When you reach the end of the path, give the doll a hug and say, "Woof, woof."

- Keep repeating the game with different animals. A cat, a cow, a duck, and a pig all make sounds that your two-year-old will love.

Stop and Go

- Cut two paper circles (one red and one green) for your child to hold.

- Say, "It's time to run (or any other movement). Can you hold the green circle and run with me?"

- After running a bit, say, "It's time to stop. Can you hold up the red circle so we can stop?"

- To play this game another way, draw and cut out a stop sign. Use it to signal when to stop.

- Use this game to teach your child about traffic lights and stop signs.

Grand Old Duke of Teddy

- "The Grand Old Duke of York" is a fun poem to act out. It's even more fun when your child adds his teddy bear (or any other stuffed animal).

- Ask your child to hold his teddy in his arms and do the actions to the following rhyme:

> *The grand old Duke of York,*
> *He had ten thousand men.*
> *He marched them up the hill and then, (hold teddy in*
> *   the air)*
> *He marched them down again. (bring teddy down)*
> *Now when you're up, you're up, (hold teddy up)*
> *And when you're down, you're down, (bring teddy down)*
> *But when you're only halfway up, (hold teddy in the middle)*
> *You're neither up (bring teddy up)*
> *Nor down. (bring teddy down)*

- Try saying the rhyme faster and faster, then slower and slower.

Bear in the Cave

- Once your two-year-old has played this game, he will want to play it over and over.

- Ask your child to squat down and pretend to be in a cave. A table with a cloth hanging over the sides makes a great "cave."

- Say the words, "Bear in the cave" three times. Each time that you say it, make your voice a little louder.

- The fourth time say, "Bear out of the cave!" in a very loud voice.

- Your loud voice is the signal for your child to jump out from under the table and say, "Grrr."

- You can make up other places to play this game, such as bear in the chair, bear behind the door, and so on.

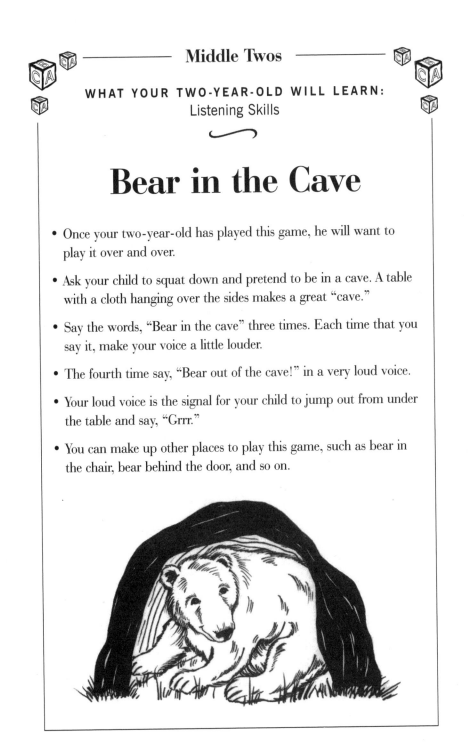

Games to Play with Two-Year-Olds

Teddy's Tired

- Chant the following.

  Teddy's tired,
  Teddy's tired,
  Go to sleep,
  Go to sleep,
  Close your little eyes,
  Close your little eyes,
  Don't make a peep,
  Don't make a peep.

- As you chant, your child and his teddy bear lie down on the floor and pretend to be asleep. Sing the last two lines very softly.

- After all is quiet for a few seconds, say in a loud voice, "Spring is here! Wake up, wake up!" Your child and his teddy bear wake up and move around the room on all fours saying, "Grrrr."

- The surprise element of this game is very appealing to a two-year-old.

Wee Willie Winkie

- "Wee Willie Winkie" is a charming nursery rhyme that children love to hear over and over.

- Recite the poem.

    Wee Willie Winkie,
    Runs through the town,
    Upstairs and downstairs
    In his nightgown.

    Rapping at the windows,
    Crying at the locks,
    "Are the children in their beds?
    For now it's eight o'clock."

- Act out the poem. Run around and gently rap at the windows.

- Say the last two lines in a loud voice.

- Lie down and pretend to be sleeping.

- Practice this rhyme with your two-year-old and try to get him to say the last line with you. He will particularly enjoy lying down and pretending to sleep.

Little Bo Peep

- The nursery rhyme "Little Bo Peep" is a lot of fun to act out.

- First say the rhyme with your child a few times so that he will be familiar with it.

  Little Bo Peep has lost her sheep
  And can't tell where to find them.
  Leave them alone, and they'll come home,
  Wagging their tails behind them.

- Pretend to be a sheep and say, "Baa, baa."

- Play a hiding game. Hide behind a door or chair and say, "Baa, baa." Your child will come to find you.

- Play another game with this rhyme. Put a shoebox on the floor and show your child how to jump over the box.

- Pretend that you are sheep coming home. Jump over the box as you say "Baa, baa" and run around the room.

Clap Your Hands

- Show your two-year-old all the different ways that his body can move, such as stamping feet, clapping hands, shaking hips, nodding head, shaking fingers, and bending knees.

- Sing this folk song and do the actions with your child.

> *Clap, clap, clap your hands,*
> *Clap your hands together.*
> *Clap, clap, clap your hands,*
> *Clap your hands together.*
>
> *Stamp, stamp, stamp your feet…*
> *Shake, shake, shake your hips…*
> *Bend, bend, bend your knees…*

WHAT YOUR TWO-YEAR-OLD WILL LEARN:
Fun

Swing Me Over

- Say this poem while holding your child in your arms, swinging him back and forth, or pushing him in a swing. Use a singsong voice or make up your own tune.

  Swing me over the water,
  Swing me over the sea,
  Swing me over the garden wall,
  And swing me home for tea.

  Swing me over the treetops,
  Swing me over the zoo,
  Swing me over the garden
  * wall,*
  And swing me back to you!

- On the words "Swing me back to you," give your child a big hug.

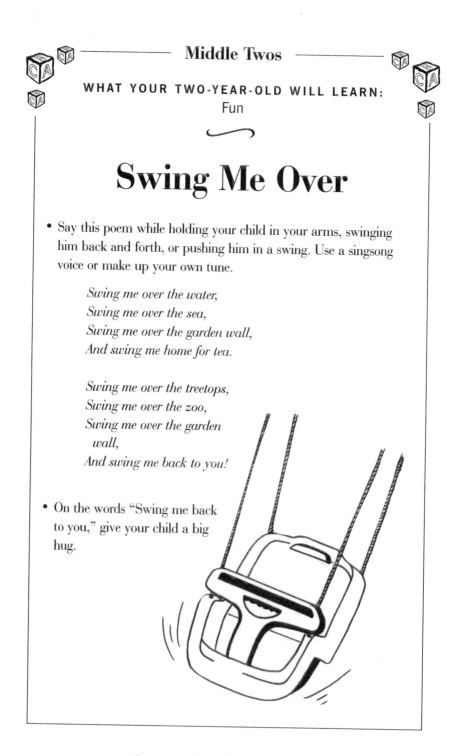

Ride a Cock Horse

- Recite the poem "Ride a Cock Horse" to your two-year-old.

  Ride a cock horse to Banbury Cross,
  To see a fine lady upon a white horse.
  Rings on her fingers and bells on her toes,
  She shall have music wherever she goes.

- As you recite the poem, pretend to ride around the room on a horse. If you have a stick horse, that would add to the fun.

- Next time, ask your child to ride his horse with you. On the words "She shall have music wherever she goes," ride your horses to a different room.

- When you get to the new room, sing one of your favorite songs.

  - "Twinkle, Twinkle, Little Star"
  - "Mary Had a Little Lamb"
  - "The Wheels on the Bus"

- Keep repeating the poem, and each time, ride to a new place and "have music wherever you go."

I Don't Care

- Chant the following and do the actions with your two-year-old.

    Shake your arm and I don't care,
    Shake your arm and I don't care,
    Shake your arm and I don't care,
    Shake it every day.

    Shake your leg and I don't care,
    Shake your leg and I don't care,
    Shake your leg and I don't care,
    Shake it every day.

- Here are more ideas to expand the chant.

    Wave your arm...
    Jump up and down...
    Bump your hips...
    Swing your arms...
    March, march, march...

See the Little Ducklings

- Fingerplays develop different capacities of the brain. Doing movement and language together draws on both sides of the brain.

- Recite this poem with your child and do the actions.

  *See the little ducklings, (make a duck bill with the heel of
  your palms together)*
  Swimming here and there. (move your palms back and forth)
  *Heads are in the water, (make a headfirst diving motion with
  your hands)*
  *Tails are in the air. (put your hands behind your back and
  wiggle them like a tail)*

- You can also act out this poem.

Finger Puppets

- Fingers make wonderful puppets. All you have to do is draw on them.

- Use a marker to make faces of any kind.

- Draw two eyes, a nose, and a mouth on each finger of one hand.

- Recite the poem "Five Little Monkeys" as you wiggle one finger at a time.

    Five little monkeys jumping on the bed,
    One fell off and hurt his little head.
    Mama called the doctor, and the doctor said,
    "No more monkeys jumping on the bed!"

- Draw on your child's fingers and encourage him to say the poem with you.

Eggs

- Enjoy this simple fingerplay with your two-year-old.

- Recite the poem and hold up the correct finger.

    Mommy bought an egg. (little finger)
    Daddy cracked it open. (ring finger)
    Sister put it in the pan. (middle finger)
    Brother cooked it. (index finger)
    And this little fellow ate it all up. (thumb)

- Use the names of friends, relatives, and even favorite animals.

- Talk about all the different ways that you can cook eggs. Choose one way—over-easy, hard-boiled, poached, or scrambled—and show your child how to cook the egg.

WHAT YOUR TWO-YEAR-OLD WILL LEARN:
Language Skills

Is This the Choo Choo Train?

- Call-and-response chants are wonderful vehicles for developing language.

- In the following chant, the child's response will always be the same two words: "Oh, yes." At first, say the words "Oh, yes" with him.

> *Is this the choo choo train?*
> *Oh, yes.*
> *Does it chug along?*
> *Oh, yes.*
> *Choo, choo, choo,*
> *Oh, yes.*
> *Let's choo choo to the kitchen,*
> *Oh, yes.*
> *Let's choo choo to the door,*
> *Oh, yes.*

- Chug along like a train as you say the words and keep choo, chooing until your child tires of the game.

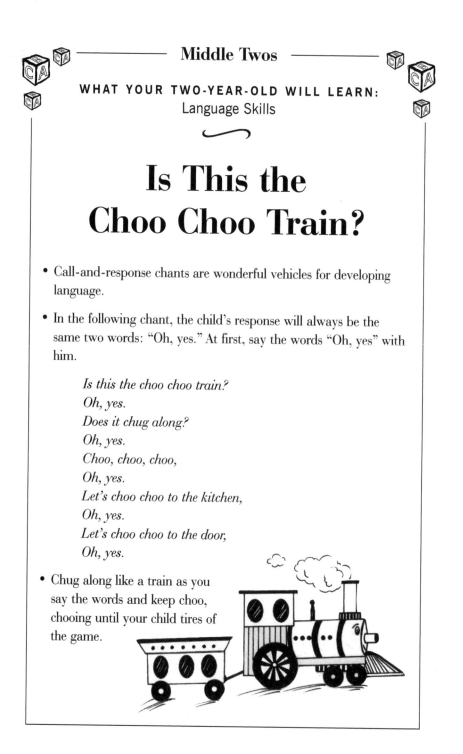

No, No, No

- Two-year-olds love to assert themselves with the word "no." This game can turn a stressful situation into a more relaxed and humorous one.

- Shake your head "no" as you say:

    No, no, no.
    I like to say, "no,
    No, no, no."
    I like to say, "no,
    No, no, no, no, no,
    No, no, no, no, no,
    No, no, no."
    I like to say, "no."

- Your child will quickly join you in this little game.

- Show him how to shake his finger at the same time that he is saying, "No." Shake your head up and down and repeat with the word "Yes."

Bears Eat Honey

- Say the following rhyme with your child:

    Bears eat honey,
    Cows eat corn,
    What do you eat when you get up in the morn?

- Talk about what you eat for breakfast.

- Repeat the rhyme starting with your child's name. Keep everything else the same.

    _____ *(child's name) eats toast,*
    Cows eat corn, etc.

- Talk about different animals and what they eat. Start the rhyme
  with a different first line and keep everything else the same.

    Dogs eat bones....
    Rabbits eat carrots....
    Monkeys eat bananas....
    Babies eat oatmeal....

I Had a Little Turtle

- This familiar poem is a particular favorite with two-year-olds.

- Show your child pictures of turtles or, better yet, find a real one to observe.

> *There was a little turtle that lived in a box,*
> *He swam in the water,*
> *And he climbed on the rocks.*
> *He snapped at a mosquito,*
> *He snapped at a flea,*
> *He snapped at a minnow,*
> *And he snapped at me.*
>
> *He caught the mosquito,*
> *He caught the flea,*
> *He caught the minnow,*
> *But he didn't catch me!*

Peter Piper

- Two-year-old children are too young to say tongue twisters, but they love to hear them.

- Listening to a tongue twister helps them learn about sounds.

- Peter Piper is a good nursery rhyme for making the "p" sound familiar.

- As you say the tongue twister, accent the "p" sound on each word. You will soon hear your two-year-old repeating the sound over and over.

> *Peter Piper picked a peck of pickled peppers.*
> *A peck of pickled peppers, Peter Piper picked.*
> *If Peter Piper picked a peck of pickled peppers,*
> *Where's the peck of pickled peppers Peter Piper picked?*

Diddle Diddle Dumpling

- Recite this popular nursery rhyme.

   Diddle diddle dumpling,
   My son John (hop on one foot)
   Went to bed with his stockings on.
   One shoe off, (point to one foot)
   One shoe on, (point to the other foot)
   Diddle diddle dumpling,
   My son John. (hop on one foot)

- Put one shoe on your child's foot. Repeat the poem and point to the foot with one shoe on and the one with one shoe off.

- Now put on both shoes. When you come to the words "One shoe off," take off one shoe.

Hickory Dickory Dock

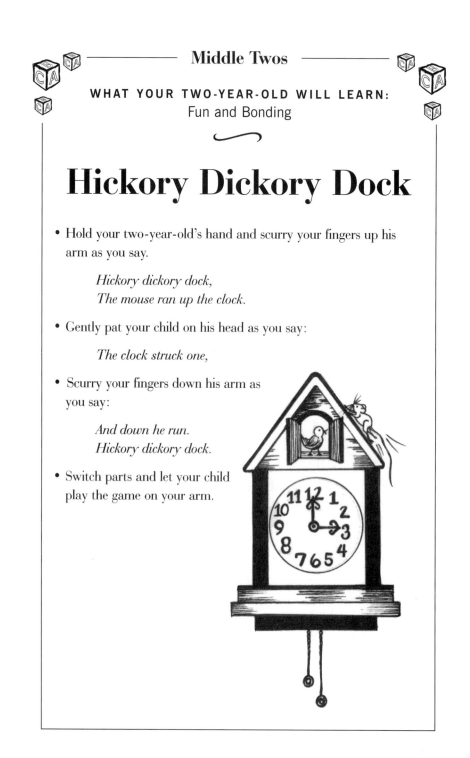

- Hold your two-year-old's hand and scurry your fingers up his arm as you say.

    Hickory dickory dock,
    The mouse ran up the clock.

- Gently pat your child on his head as you say:

    The clock struck one,

- Scurry your fingers down his arm as you say:

    And down he run.
    Hickory dickory dock.

- Switch parts and let your child play the game on your arm.

Singathon

- Singing is a wonderful activity.

- Talk about songs that your child knows. He may know more than you realize.

- Practice two or three of the songs together. Tell him that when you get into the car, you are going to sing those songs.

- Once inside the car, remind your two-year-old of the songs you are going to sing.

- Say "One, two, ready, sing!" Have a great time!

AUTHOR NOTE: I've known children who refused to sing a particular song unless they were in the car.

WHAT YOUR TWO-YEAR-OLD WILL LEARN:
Creativity

Sticker Fun

- Two-year-olds love stickers, so games that use stickers keep their attention.

- Take two tongue depressors and put a sticker on the end of each to create sticker puppets.

- Hold one sticker puppet in each hand. Put your hands behind your back.

- Bring one hand from behind your back, moving the stick up and down while you sing one of your child's favorite songs.

- Ask your child, "Would you like to see another puppet?" Bring out the other hand and move it up and down while you sing a different song.

- Give the sticker puppets to your child and let him try to play the game.

Rain Songs

• Get dressed in your rain clothes, go outside, and sing or recite rain songs and poems.

It's raining, it's pouring,
The old man is snoring.
He went to bed and bumped his head,
And he didn't get up until morning.

Slip on your raincoat,
Put on your galoshes,
Wading in the puddles
Makes splishes and sploshes.

Rain, rain, go away,
Come again another day.
Little _____ [child's name] wants to play,
Rain, rain, go away.

Rain, rain, falling on the ground,
Pitter, patter, what a lovely sound.
Rain, rain, falling on my nose,
Drip, drip, drip, drip,
Squooshing in my toes.

Dr. Foster went to Gloucester
In a shower of rain.
He stepped in a puddle
Right up to his middle
And never went there again.

The Muffin Man

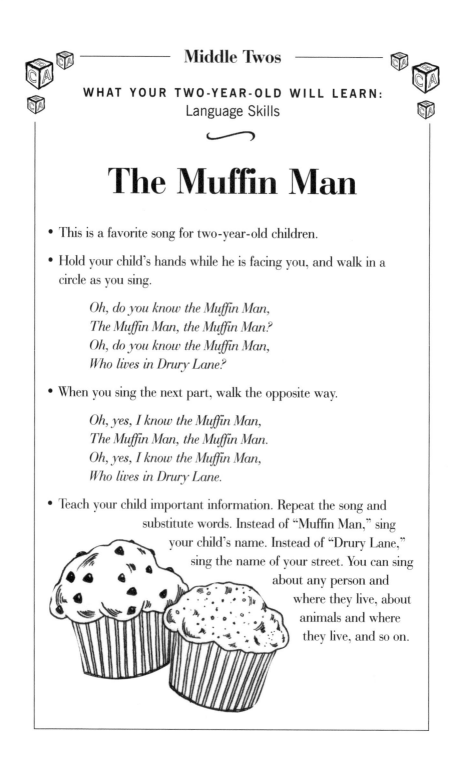

- This is a favorite song for two-year-old children.

- Hold your child's hands while he is facing you, and walk in a circle as you sing.

    Oh, do you know the Muffin Man,
    The Muffin Man, the Muffin Man?
    Oh, do you know the Muffin Man,
    Who lives in Drury Lane?

- When you sing the next part, walk the opposite way.

    Oh, yes, I know the Muffin Man,
    The Muffin Man, the Muffin Man.
    Oh, yes, I know the Muffin Man,
    Who lives in Drury Lane.

- Teach your child important information. Repeat the song and substitute words. Instead of "Muffin Man," sing your child's name. Instead of "Drury Lane," sing the name of your street. You can sing about any person and where they live, about animals and where they live, and so on.

Games with Toys

- Young children enjoy playing simple games such as "Ring Around the Rosy."

- Playing the game with a stuffed animal reinforces the rules of the game.

- Hold a favorite stuffed animal in your arms. Give your child another favorite to hold in his arms.

- Sing the song "Ring Around the Rosie" and when you come to the "fall down" part, fall down.

- Now take it one step further. Sit on the floor and make the stuffed animal dance with your hands. When you come to the "fall down" part, let the toy fall to the ground.

- Two-year-olds love this game so much that they might play it without you.

- One of the many good things about this game is that your little one learns to wait for the words "fall down."

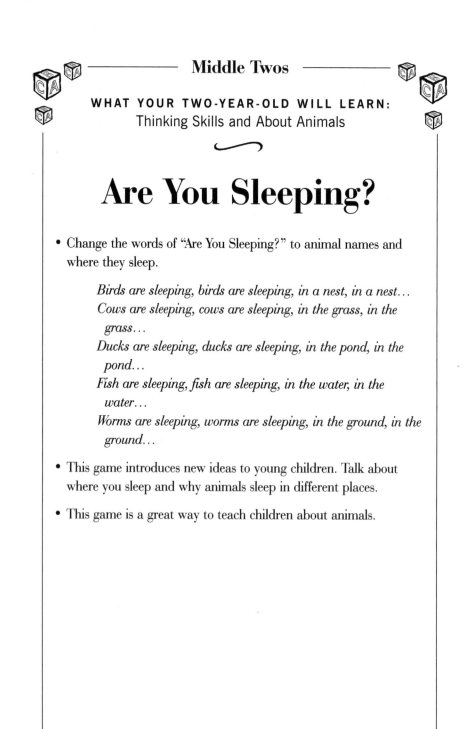

Are You Sleeping?

- Change the words of "Are You Sleeping?" to animal names and where they sleep.

  Birds are sleeping, birds are sleeping, in a nest, in a nest...
  Cows are sleeping, cows are sleeping, in the grass, in the grass...
  Ducks are sleeping, ducks are sleeping, in the pond, in the pond...
  Fish are sleeping, fish are sleeping, in the water, in the water...
  Worms are sleeping, worms are sleeping, in the ground, in the ground...

- This game introduces new ideas to young children. Talk about where you sleep and why animals sleep in different places.

- This game is a great way to teach children about animals.

The Whisper Game

- Two-year-olds are fascinated with whispering. They love experimenting with ways to change their voices.

- Say to your child in a normal voice, "I love you." Then say the same words in a whisper.

- Ask your child if he can say, "I love you" in a whisper.

- This may take a little practice, but soon he will understand.

- Ask questions in a whisper. "What does the cow say?" "What does the duck say?"

- Encourage him to whisper the answer. If he answers in a normal voice, whisper the answer yourself.

- Try singing a favorite song in a whisper, such as "Twinkle, Twinkle, Little Star" or "The ABC Song."

Rebus Stories

- A rebus is a picture that represents a word. The ancient Egyptians told stories using pictures this way.

- Tell a story about what your two-year-old likes to do. Begin with a short story, about two or three sentences long.

- Cut the rebus pictures from magazines or draw them. Coloring books are also excellent sources for pictures.

- At the beginning, only use one or two pictures in the story.

- Identify the pictures and tell the story. For example, with a picture of a dog and a swing, your story could be:

    Once upon a time there was a little boy named _____ [child's name]. He had a dog named _____ [dog's name]. They went outside to play on the swing.

- Write the story on paper and put the pictures of the dog and the swing where those words should be.

- Read the story to your child, touching each word as you say it.

- Rebus stories introduce children to the mechanics of reading, following the text from left to right and top to bottom.

The Gingerbread Man

- Tell your own version of "The Gingerbread Man." A two-year-old's attention span is very short, so the story should be, too.

  Once upon a time there was a little gingerbread man who loved to run. After breakfast he would say, "Run, run, as fast as you can. You can't catch me, I'm the gingerbread man."

- Each time you say the words "Run, run," take your child's hand and run in a circle. Continue the story, adding about two sentences at a time.

  The gingerbread man went to see his grandma, and when he got there he said, "Run, run, as fast as you can. You can't catch me, I'm the gingerbread man."

- Soon your two-year-old will understand that whenever he hears "Run, run," it's time for him to run.

- This game is good for transitions. When it's time to go outside, he can "run, run" to the door.

Car Book

- In magazines or catalogs, find pictures of cars in different places such as on the street, on the highway, in a store, and so on.

- Cut out the pictures and glue them onto heavy paper.

- Staple the pages together to make a book about cars for your two-year-old.

- Give your child his car book, and as he turns the pages, ask questions about the book.
  - Can you find a red car?
  - Can you find a car on the street?
  - Does the car have wheels?
  - Can you find a funny car?

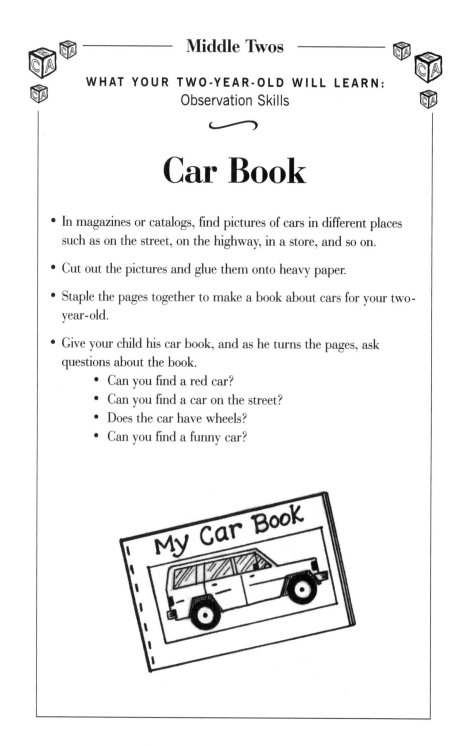

Happy, Sad Animals

- Your two-year-old loves to make animal sounds.

- Ask your two-year-old, "What could make a dog very happy?" The answers could be a new bone, lots of hugs, playing a game, and so on.

- Pretend to bark with a happy sound.

- Ask your child, "What could make a dog sad?" The answers could be no one to play with, not able to find a bone, and so on.

- Try barking sadly.

- Continue this game with other animal sounds that are familiar to your two-year-old.

Happy or Sad?

- Look through magazines with your child and talk about the expressions on people's faces.

- Point out happy faces and sad faces.

- Make a happy face and then a sad face. Ask your two-year-old to do the same.

- Tell your child some things that make you happy.
    - I am happy when I give you a hug.
    - I am happy when we play together.

- Tell your child some things that make you sad.
    - I am sad when a toy gets broken.
    - I am sad when you are sad.

Spoon Talk

- Find a small plastic spoon that is easy for your child to hold.

- Use markers to draw a happy face on one side and a sad face on the other.

- Hold up the happy side and say, "I'm so happy, ha, ha, ha, ha, ha." Give the spoon to your child and ask him to repeat what you said.

- Hold up the sad face and say, "I'm so sad, boo hoo, boo hoo." Give the spoon to your child and ask him to repeat what you said.

- Talk about things you can say when you are happy or sad and the different facial expressions that show happiness or sadness.

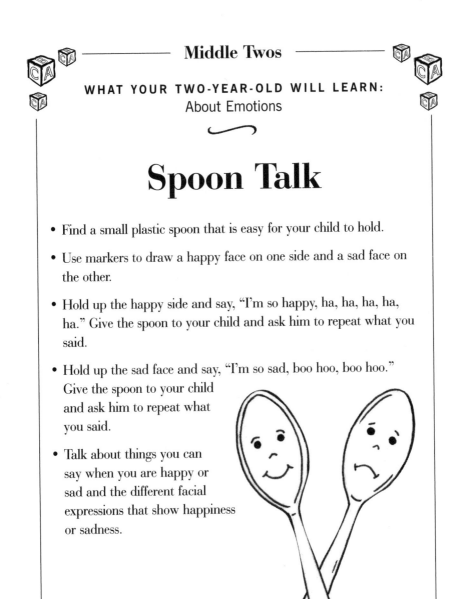

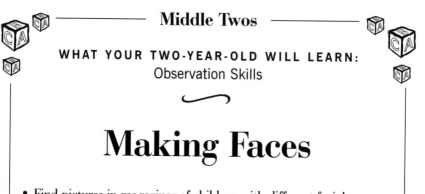

Making Faces

- Find pictures in magazines of children with different facial expressions. Cut out the pictures and show them to your child.

- Talk about each picture and then try to make the same expression on your face.

- Ask your child to make the same expression on his face.

- Look for pictures of happy faces, silly faces, sad faces, or mad faces.

- Look for pictures with children doing physical activities, such as standing on one leg, bending over, or running. Then do the activity with your child.

A Glove Story

- Find a gardening glove or any glove that you do not mind drawing on. (This is a great game for using up single gloves that have lost their partners.)

- Draw faces on the fingertips with a marker and name them. They can be members of your family, animals, or anything else.

- Put the glove on your hand and introduce the characters to your two-year-old.

- As you introduce each finger, tell who it is and say something in that person's or animal's voice. For example, "This is Mr. Cow. Moo, moo."

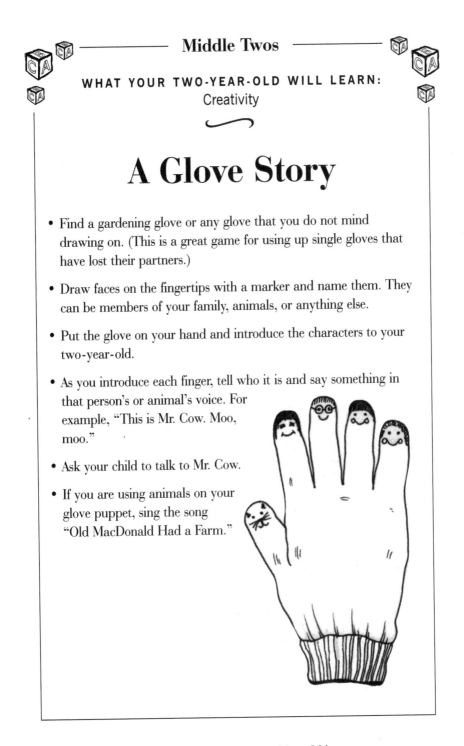

- Ask your child to talk to Mr. Cow.

- If you are using animals on your glove puppet, sing the song "Old MacDonald Had a Farm."

WHAT YOUR TWO-YEAR-OLD WILL LEARN:
Self-Esteem

When I Was a Baby

- Children love to learn about themselves as babies. This helps them feel important and special.

- Use a special book or box for your child to collect photos, birthday and holiday cards, artwork, and anything else you or your child would like to include.

- Other things that you could include in this book:
  - Newspaper ads with his favorite foods.
  - Newspapers published on his birthday.
  - Hand- and footprints of you and him at different ages.
  - Favorite toys as they are outgrown.

- You and your child will enjoy these memories for many years to come.

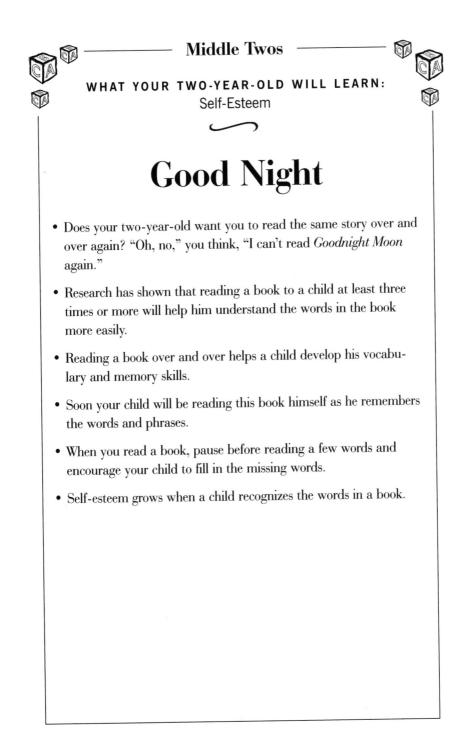

Good Night

- Does your two-year-old want you to read the same story over and over again? "Oh, no," you think, "I can't read *Goodnight Moon* again."

- Research has shown that reading a book to a child at least three times or more will help him understand the words in the book more easily.

- Reading a book over and over helps a child develop his vocabulary and memory skills.

- Soon your child will be reading this book himself as he remembers the words and phrases.

- When you read a book, pause before reading a few words and encourage your child to fill in the missing words.

- Self-esteem grows when a child recognizes the words in a book.

Making Sentences

- Two- and three-word sentences develop your child's language skills and are important pre-reading experiences.

- Start with simple sentences about a familiar theme, such as toys.
    - I like balls.
    - I like blocks.
    - I like _____. (Let your child fill in the next word.)

- Repeat the last sentence and encourage your child to fill in new words.

- Change the theme of the sentences, but say, "I like" before each word.

- Name familiar relatives, friends, animals, or food.

- The next step is to add descriptive words. "I like red balls." "I like big blocks."

Find Your Name

- Print your child's name on several index cards.

- Print each card in a different color.

- Hide the cards in different places in the room. Under a sofa, behind a couch, or behind a door are all good hiding places. Be sure most of the card is visible.

- Walk around the room with your two-year-old to find the name cards.

Nature's Treasures

- A walk in the outdoors is always full of fascinating things to see and hear.

- Two-year-olds are so curious, they want to examine every leaf, stick, and stone. This is a perfect opportunity to bring back treasures that you can continue to enjoy for a long time. Gather together your child's favorite rocks (small ones), leaves, and sticks (small ones).

  CAUTION: Supervise closely because young children may put objects in their mouths.

- Place contact paper on a wall or table with the sticky side out. Let your child stick his treasures on the paper to create a beautiful picture about nature. He will admire and talk about his picture for a long time.

- Your two-year-old will also discover that if he removes the objects from the paper a couple of times, the paper will lose its stickiness.

Measure the Sunflowers

- Sunflowers often grow as high as 10 feet, at a rate of about 6 inches a week.

- Attach a large piece of paper to the wall.

- Plant sunflower seeds and carefully water them as needed.

- Once a week, measure the growth and mark the sunflower plant's height on the wall chart. Compare it to your child's height.

- Ask your child to make a mark or draw something on the chart at the height of the sunflower.

- In a few weeks, measure the plant and your child again. By charting the growth, he will begin to understand that the flower is actually growing.

- Compare it to his growth over the same period.

Spring Is Coming

- The first signs of spring are always exciting. To see a blade of grass peeping through the ground or hear a bird chirping always reminds us of the wonder of nature.

- Walk outside with your two-year-old and look at all the signs of spring.

Butterflies and Caterpillars

- Read books about caterpillars and look for pictures in magazines as well.

- Look for pictures of butterflies in books and magazines.

- Search outdoors for caterpillars and butterflies.

- Talk about how caterpillars become butterflies.

Hot Summer Fun

- Go outside in a bathing suit or clothing that is okay to get wet.

- Turn on a sprinkler, preferably one that turns in a circle.

- Explain to your two-year-old how the water moves in a circle. Help him to anticipate when the water is coming.

- Start by putting an arm or a leg in the water when it comes to you. Keep adding more parts of the body.

- Another sprinkler game is chasing the water as the sprinkler turns.

- Play a game with a hose. Turn it on so that the water is a soft and gentle stream.

- Let your child fill containers, wash the trees, get you wet, and just have fun.

Rocks

- Looking for rocks is a wonderful way to satisfy your two-year-old's natural curiosity.

- Find a box for rock collecting. A shoebox works very well.

- Go on a rock hunt. Your child will love finding rocks and putting them into the box.

- When you return home, there are several things that you can do with the rocks.
    - Wash the rocks. Give your child a pan of water and a sponge, and he will be thrilled. Lay them on paper towels to dry.
    - Pick up each rock and talk about how it feels. Is it smooth? Is it bumpy?
    - Sort the rocks in different ways, such as by size, by color, by shape, or by texture.

- Your child will treasure the rocks for a long time and enjoy them over and over.

Cookie Cutter Prints

- Cookie cutters have wonderful shapes for art projects.

  CAUTION: Cookie cutters can have sharp edges. Supervise closely.

- You will need a large piece of paper and some tempera paint.

- Show your two-year-old how to dip the cookie cutter into the paint and then "stamp" the piece of paper.

- He will love filling the paper with these prints.

Cotton Ball Art

- Place a large piece of colored construction paper on a table.

- You will also need a package of triple-size cotton balls and paste or a glue stick.

- Put paste or glue on a cotton ball and show your child how to stick the cotton ball onto the paper.

- You and your child can do this activity together. This will encourage language development and bonding.

- Two-year-olds get a lot of satisfaction from this game and are very proud of the finished product.

- Hang the cotton ball picture at your two-year-old's height.

Rain Art

- On a day when rain is predicted, help your two-year-old place a large piece of butcher paper outdoors on the ground.

- Put small blobs of different colors of tempera paint all over the paper.

- Wait for the rain and watch what happens to the paint.

- Bring the paper inside before all the paint has washed away.

- You will see all kinds of interesting designs and shapes.

Draw Me

- Watching you draw encourages your two-year-old's creativity. Your level of ability is not important, but your enthusiasm is.

- Tell your child what you are going to draw—him or your pet or something else. When you are finished, talk about the drawing.

- Gently outline your child's facial features with your finger. As you go around each feature, name it.

- When you are finished, draw the same features on your paper and repeat the names.

- For example, say, "I am drawing your eyes," and ask your child to touch his eyes. Say, "I am drawing your mouth," and ask your child to touch his mouth.

- Give your child paper and crayons and encourage him to draw his own creations.

Number Art

- Sit with your child and look through magazines for numbers. It is best to start with the numbers 1 and 2. Catalogs, magazines, and calendars are good sources.

- Each time you see a 1 or a 2, point to it and say its name.

- Cut out lots of these numbers.

- Your child can help you glue them onto a piece of construction paper. Each time you glue on a number, name it.

- Hang the collage in a prominent place so that your child can look at it often.

Painting

- Your two-year-old is ready to experiment with tempera paint.

- Small pieces of sponge held by spring-type clothespins make wonderful paintbrushes.

- Leaves and feathers are great fun to explore as paintbrushes.

- Painting experiences will boost your child's self-esteem.

Roly-Poly Sandwiches

- Cut the crusts off two slices of whole wheat bread.

- Put peanut butter, jelly, honey, and cinnamon on the table.

- Show your child how to use a rolling pin to flatten the bread.

- Ask your child to spread peanut butter on the bread and to choose whatever else he would like to put on it.

- While he is spreading his bread, spread yours to model the process.

- Help your child roll up the sandwich like a jellyroll.

- Cut the roll into three or four slices. Your two-year-old will be fascinated with the design in the middle and will love eating the sandwich.

Oh Boy, Kebabs!

- Select several of your child's favorite fruits and vegetables and cut them into chunks.

- Use apples, bananas, pears, cucumbers, carrots, celery, straw-berries, and any other fruit or vegetable that is skewered easily.

- Show your child how to make a kebab by threading the chunks onto a wooden skewer or long toothpick.

- As he puts the pieces onto the skewer, name the fruit or vegetable and say something positive about it. For exam-ple: "That's an apple. It tastes sweet and crunchy."

- When your child hears you describe a fruit or vegetable in a positive way, he will develop a positive attitude about it.

Pumpkin Fun

- Carving a pumpkin is always a lot of fun for everyone. Your two-year-old will delight in seeing the inside of a pumpkin as well as the face that you carve.

- Before or after carving the pumpkin's face, scoop out the inside of the pumpkin and save the seeds for another treat.

- With your child's help, wash the pumpkin seeds and put them on a cookie sheet to dry.

- Bake them in a 300° oven for about 20 minutes or until they are brown.

- Let your two-year-old shake a little bit of salt on the seeds. Eat them and enjoy!

Rudolph Sandwich

- Everyone will enjoy making a "Rudolph the Red-Nosed Reindeer" treat.

- Cut a piece of bread into two triangles.

- Let your child spread the triangles with butter, peanut butter, or cream cheese.

- Stick pretzels into the bread for antlers.

- Put out a variety of items for eyes, nose, and mouth such as raisins, pepper slices, olives, tomatoes (for the nose) and nuts. Let your two-year-old decide which to use.

- When you are finished, sing the song "Rudolph the Red-Nosed Reindeer."

Food Textures

- Pour some raisins and pretzels in a dish.

- Pick up a raisin and put it in your mouth. Give one to your child to put in his mouth.

- Say words such as "soft" and "chewy" when you are finished eating the raisin.

- Now pick up a pretzel. Say words such as "hard" and "crunchy" when are you finished eating the pretzel.

- Give a raisin or a pretzel to your child. Ask him if it is soft or hard, chewy, or crunchy.

- Encourage your child to put the crunchy pretzel in his mouth.

- Pour several pretzels and raisins in a dish and let your child sort them.

Vegetable Shopping

- Go to the supermarket and buy ingredients to make soup.

- Buy carrots, onions, tomatoes, canned chicken broth, and celery.

- Read the book *Stone Soup* by Marcia Brown.

- Make soup with your child. Use the ingredients that you purchased at the market. Add some seasonings and let it cook until
  the carrots get soft.

- Strain the soup and eat with crackers.

A Street of Blocks

- Two-year-olds enjoy putting blocks side by side.

- Encourage your child to make a long line of blocks. Tell him that you are making a street for the car to drive on.

- Get a toy car and push it along the block road.

- Your child will want to push the cars along the road when he sees you doing it.

- Get more toy cars and trucks and push them along the road. Pretend to beep the horn and say, "Look out, here I come!"

- Add other blocks and stand them upright. These can be houses, buildings, the supermarket, or whatever you imagine.

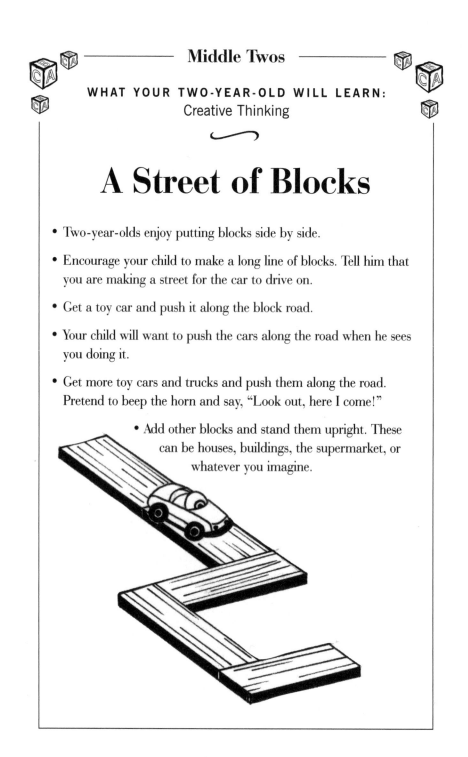

Boxing Practice

- Find three boxes of different sizes with separate lids. Shoeboxes are good for this activity.

- Decorate each box and its lid with stickers, making sure that the stickers on the box and the lid match. Use different stickers for each box.

- Show the boxes to your child with the lids on.

- Ask your two-year-old to take off the lids.

- Now ask him to put the lids back on again.

- He will probably try to put a lid on a box that it does not fit. When he discovers the correct box, praise his problem-solving skills.

- Talk about the stickers on the boxes. Show him that the tops and bottoms have the same stickers.

Put the Bear...

- Understanding the position of things develops your child's language. These relationship words help your two-year-old string words and ideas together.

- Place your child's teddy bear on a chair and say, "The bear is *on* the chair."

- Put the bear under the chair and say, "The bear is *under* the chair."

- Ask your child to put the bear on the chair, then under the chair.

- Try other directions.
    - Put the bear in front of the car. (use a toy car)
    - Put the bear behind the car.
    - Put the bear next to the table.

The Sorting Game

- This game encourages two-year-olds to clean up their toys and teaches them matching skills at the same time.

- Pick one category, such as blocks, and search for blocks all over the room or house. Your child will enjoy this very much. Make it fun by saying, "Block, block, where are you?" "Oh, here you are!"

- Put all of the blocks into a container.

- Try matching the blocks by size. Pick one block and ask your child to find another of the same size.

- You can also match blocks by color.

- When you have finished with blocks, start looking for other toys.

Dressing Up

- Put dress-up things in a box.

- Scarves, neckties, hats, and jewelry all work well, and your child will enjoy them very much.

- To get things started, put a scarf over your shoulder and a hat on your head. Change the tone or accent of your voice.

- Let your two-year-old try on whatever is in the box. He may put it on backwards or upside down. No matter, encourage and compliment his choice of dress-ups.

- When you compliment him about his choices, he will feel that his ideas are valuable.

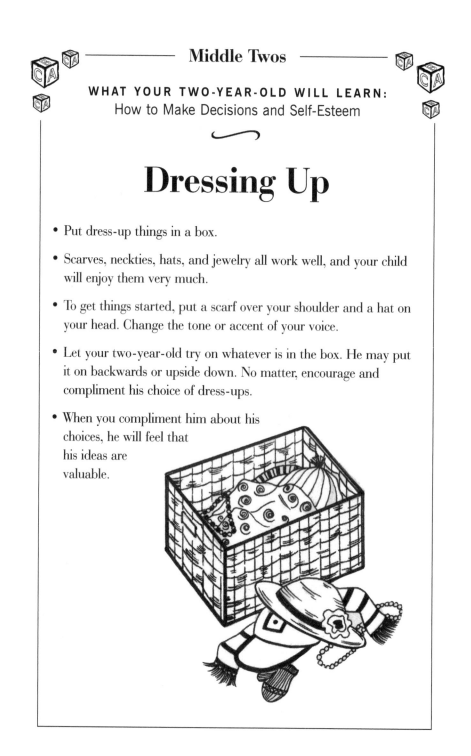

Getting Into Shapes

- You will need blocks of different shapes, such as circles, squares, and triangles to play this game.

- Give your child the square block and let him hold it and feel its shape. Talk about its name and point out other square shapes in the room.

- Give your child another block of a different shape. Talk about this shape.

- Take the first and second blocks and place them into a sack or large bag.

- Hold another square block in your hand. Show it to him and ask him to find the matching shape in the sack.

- At first, he can put his hand into the sack and look at what he takes out. As he gets better at the game, encourage him to identify the shape by feeling the block.

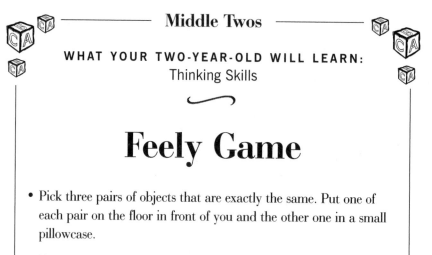

WHAT YOUR TWO-YEAR-OLD WILL LEARN:
Thinking Skills

Feely Game

- Pick three pairs of objects that are exactly the same. Put one of each pair on the floor in front of you and the other one in a small pillowcase.

- Encourage your child to reach into the pillowcase and pick out one object. Ask him to put it next to the other one on the floor.

- Once your two-year-old can do this, ask him to reach in the pillowcase without looking and touch one of the objects. Then ask him to find an object on the floor that feels the same. When he has guessed, let him take the object out of the pillowcase to see if it matches.

- When your child is able to do this easily, try this with three new objects.

- Suggestions for objects include two spoons, two blocks, matching pieces of material, two toothbrushes, and two sponges.

Roses Are Red

- Find pictures of roses and violets in magazines. Gardening magazines are very helpful.

- Cut out the pictures and glue each picture to a piece of heavy cardboard. It is good to have three pictures of roses and three pictures of violets.

- Show the pictures to your two-year-old and tell him the names of the flowers. Play a matching game by sorting the cards into roses and violets.

- Recite the familiar nursery rhyme.

Roses are red, (point to the roses)
Violets are blue, (point to the violets)
Sugar is sweet,
And so are you. (give your
child a big hug)

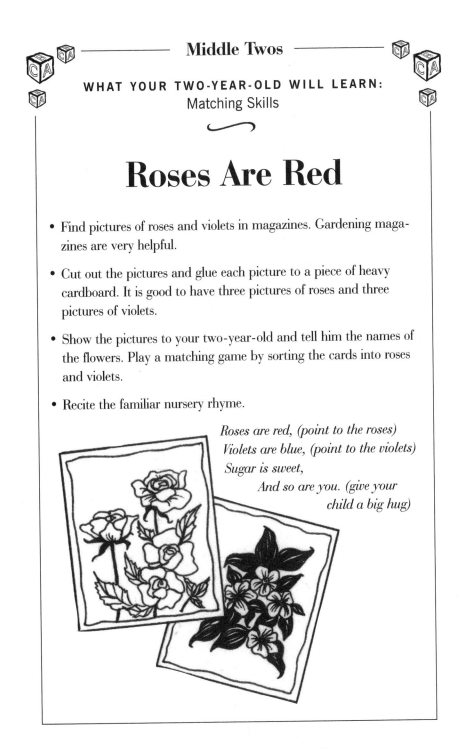

Name the Noise

- There are so many interesting noises in a two-year-old's environment. When they can identify these noises, they feel confident.

- Name sounds that you hear, such as cars, airplanes, trains, dogs barking, rain falling, thunder, vacuum cleaners, or running water.

- Make a tape recording of the familiar sounds and listen to it with your child. Name the sounds as you listen.

- Play the tape and talk about the sounds on the tape. For example, if he says that he hears a door closing, talk about how doors open and close, who might come in the door, and why we close doors.

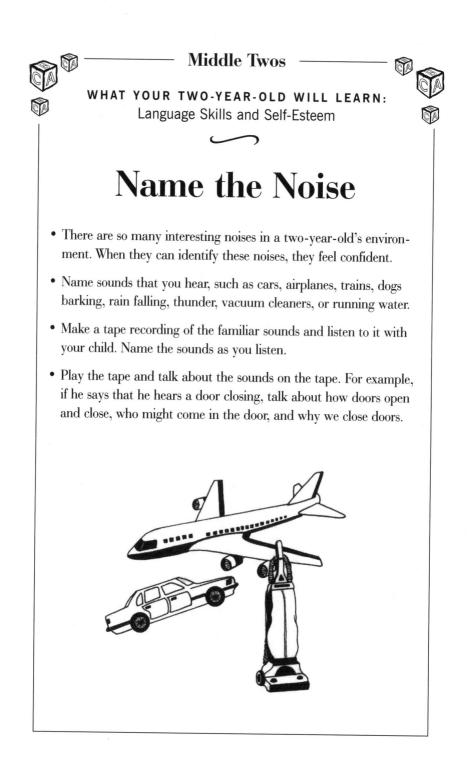

Games to Play with Two-Year-Olds

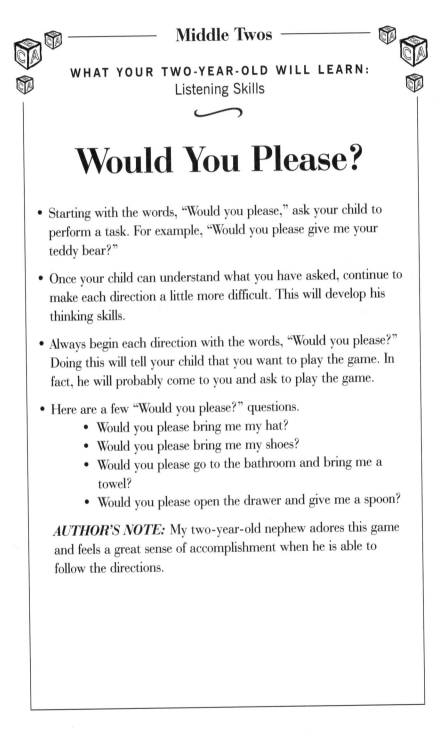

Would You Please?

- Starting with the words, "Would you please," ask your child to perform a task. For example, "Would you please give me your teddy bear?"

- Once your child can understand what you have asked, continue to make each direction a little more difficult. This will develop his thinking skills.

- Always begin each direction with the words, "Would you please?" Doing this will tell your child that you want to play the game. In fact, he will probably come to you and ask to play the game.

- Here are a few "Would you please?" questions.
  - Would you please bring me my hat?
  - Would you please bring me my shoes?
  - Would you please go to the bathroom and bring me a towel?
  - Would you please open the drawer and give me a spoon?

AUTHOR'S NOTE: My two-year-old nephew adores this game and feels a great sense of accomplishment when he is able to follow the directions.

Older Twos

WHAT YOUR TWO-YEAR-OLD WILL LEARN:
About In and Out and About Elephants

Elephants

- Look at books with pictures of elephants. The pictures in the *Babar* books are fun and will help your child recognize elephants.

- Show your child how to make elephant ears. Put your hands behind your neck and lace your fingers together loosely, keeping your elbows pointed to the side. Move your arms back and forth. Say the words "out" and "in" as you move your elbows.

- Walk around the room together and pretend you are elephants.

Jumping Jacks

- Older twos enjoy jumping very much. Learning to do jumping jacks will develop their motor skills and balance.

- Show your two-year-old how to jump and land with her feet together. Do it yourself, and then ask her to copy you.

- Jump and land with your feet apart. Again, do it first, and then ask her to copy you.

- When she can jump both ways, show her how to alternate the two.

WHAT YOUR TWO-YEAR-OLD WILL LEARN:
Imagination

Jump in the Ocean

- Designate a certain area of the room as the ocean.

- Sit on the floor next to the ocean and talk about the water. "Is the water cold?" "Can you float in the water?" "How does the water taste in your mouth?"

- Count to three very slowly and then say, "Jump in the ocean." Pretend to jump into the water.

- While you are in the "ocean," you can swim different ways, splash water on each other, and talk about the different fish that you see.

- When it's time to get out of the water, you can shake off the water, dry yourself, stretch out in the sunshine, build a sand castle, and anything else your imagination dreams up.

AUTHOR'S NOTE: My grandson and I have played this game for many hours.

Copy Me

- Say, "One, two, three, copy me."

- Jump up and down.

- Ask your child to copy you.

- Say the words again, "One, two, three, copy me."

- Do a different action such as clapping your hands.

- Ask your child to copy you.

- Continue with different body movements that your child can do.

The Rope Game

- Place a rope on the floor.

- Ask your child to step over the rope.

- Continue doing actions over the rope, such as hopping and so on.

- Turn the game into a "Follow the Leader" game, with you as the leader. Here are some things that you can do.
    - Step forward and step backward over the rope.
    - Hop to the rope and step over it.
    - Crawl under the rope.

- As your child's skills progress, raise the height of the rope by tying it between two chairs.

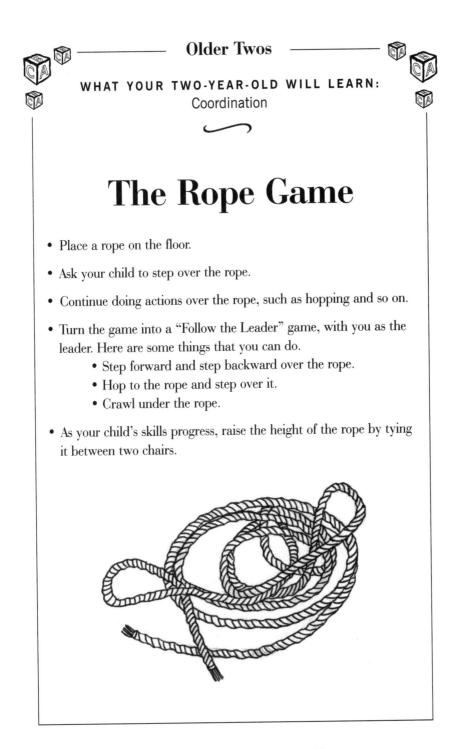

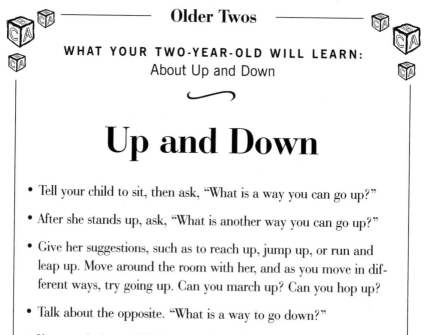

Up and Down

- Tell your child to sit, then ask, "What is a way you can go up?"

- After she stands up, ask, "What is another way you can go up?"

- Give her suggestions, such as to reach up, jump up, or run and leap up. Move around the room with her, and as you move in different ways, try going up. Can you march up? Can you hop up?

- Talk about the opposite. "What is a way to go down?"

- You can sit down, fall down, go down slowly, and jump down.

- Experiment with ways to go backward, sideways, and forward.

Blow the Wind

- Sit with your two-year-old and show her how to blow gently with her lips.

- Blow gently on her hand and ask her to blow gently on your hand.

- Recite this poem to your child.

  I can blow like the wind. (blow gently)
  I can bring the rain. (move your fingers up and down
    her arm)
  When I blow very softly,
  I can whisper your name. (whisper your child's name)

- Whispering is difficult for a two-year-old. It takes concentration and good listening skills, but the poem makes practicing fun.

Family Poems

- This takes a little effort on your part but it is definitely worth the time.

- Select several poems and rhymes that your child enjoys.

- Record different members of your family reciting these poems and rhymes.

- Each person should say only one poem.

- Play the recording for your child and see if she recognizes who is speaking.

- This is great fun and your child can enjoy the voices of her parents, siblings, grandparents, or friends at any time.

This Is the Father

- This fingerplay talks about the whole family.

- Hold up one finger at a time as you say the rhyme.

- On the last line, hold up all your fingers to represent "the family."

> *This is the father short and stout, (thumb)*
> *This is the mother with children about, (index finger)*
> *This is the brother tall you see, (middle finger)*
> *This is the sister with a toy on her knee, (ring finger)*
> *This is the baby sure to grow, (pinky)*
> *And here is the family all in a row. (all five fingers)*

- Count your fingers—1, 2, 3, 4, 5.

WHAT YOUR TWO-YEAR-OLD WILL LEARN:
Coordination

A Growing Seed

- After your child has experienced planting seeds and watching them grow, this fingerplay offers a nice reinforcement.

> *Once there was a seed in the dark, dark, ground. (hide one finger in the fist of your other hand)*
>
> *Out came the sun so big and round, (make a circle with your arms)*
>
> *Down came the rain so gentle and slow, (wiggle your fingers for the rain)*
>
> *Up came the little seed, grow, grow, grow. (push your finger through your closed fist)*

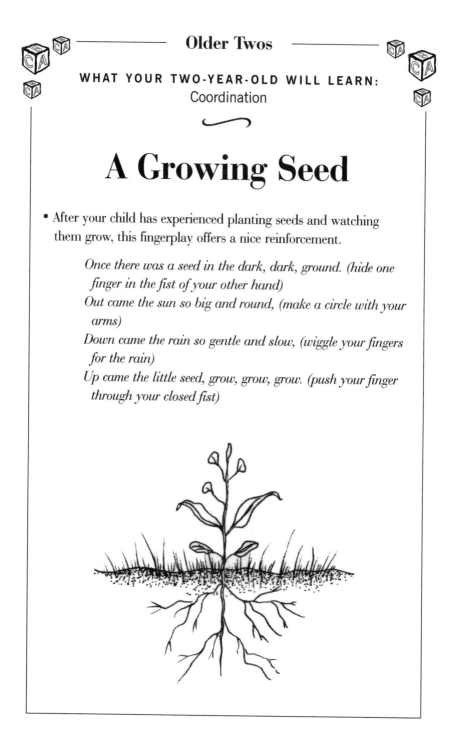

Five Little Ducks

- This poem is very popular with young children. They especially like to make the "quack, quack" sound.

- Recite the poem and do the actions.

> *Five little ducks that I once knew, (hold up five fingers)*
> *Big ones, little ones, skinny ones, too. (make big and little circles with your hands)*
> *But the one little duck with the feather on his back, (hold up one finger)*
> *All he could do was "Quack, quack, quack." (move your thumb up and down for a quacking motion)*
>
> *Down to the river they would go,*
> *Waddling, waddling, to and fro. (waddle like a duck)*
> *But the one little duck with the feather on his back, (hold up one finger)*
> *All he could do was "Quack, quack, quack."*
>
> *Up from the river they would come,*
> *With a ho, ho, ho, and a hum, hum, hum. (waddle like a duck)*
> *But the one little duck with the feather in his back, (hold up one finger)*
> *All he could do was "Quack, quack, quack."*

Furry Squirrel

- Observe squirrels with your two-year-old and talk about the squirrel's bushy tail. Show a variety of nuts to your child and tell her that nuts are a favorite food of squirrels.

- Recite the following poem and do the actions:

> *I'm a fur, fur, furry squirrel*
> *With a bush, bush, bushy tail.*
> *And I scamper here and there,*
> *Scamper everywhere,*
> *Looking for some nuts. (scamper around the room looking*
> *   for nuts)*
>
> *I've got nuts on my nose, (put a nut on your nose)*
> *Nuts on my toes, (put a nut on your toe)*
> *Nuts on my head, (put a nut on your head)*
> *Nuts in my bed, (lie down and put a nut next to your face)*
> *Nuts in my paws, (hold a nut in your hand)*
> *Nuts in my jaws. (hold a nut*
> *   up to your jaw)*
> *Crack, crack, pop!*
> *(Make a popping*
> *sound)*

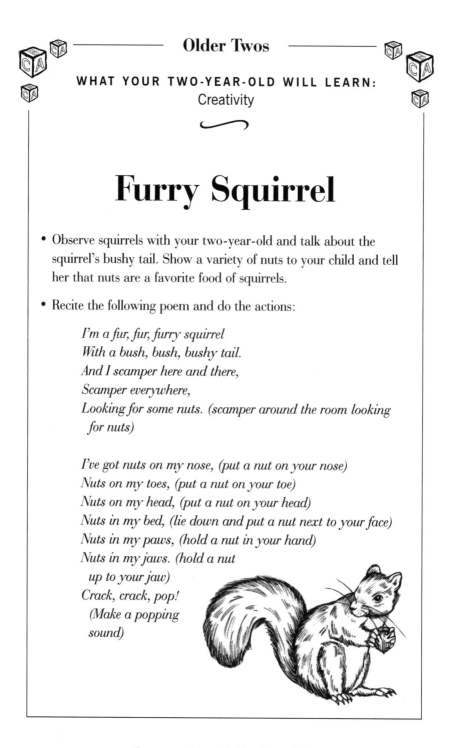

WHAT YOUR TWO-YEAR-OLD WILL LEARN:
Imitation

The Bear Hunt

- Ask your child to copy your actions.

- Sit on the floor facing your child. Start tapping your hands on the floor in a steady rhythm. Keep tapping as you say the words, unless you are performing another action.

> *Going on a bear hunt, going on a bear hunt,*
> *I'm not scared. (point to yourself and shake your head "no")*
> *Oh, look, (shade your eyes as if you see something far away)*
> *Here's a lot of rocks, let's walk through. (stand up and pretend to be walking barefoot on rocks as you say:)*
> *Ouch, ouch, ouch.*
> *Oh, look, Here's some very tall grass, let's walk through. (part the tall grass as you say the next line)*
> *Swish, swish, swish.*
> *Here comes a river, uh oh, no bridge.*
> *Let's swim across. (swim with your arms)*
> *Here comes a big tree, let's climb to the top. (move fist over fist)*
> *Oh, look, there's a great big cave. (pretend to be looking through binoculars)*
> *Let's climb down the tree and look in the cave. (climb down)*
> *Let's go in the cave. (speak in a very soft voice)*
> *Oh, look, I see two yellow eyes. (speak in a very soft and scared voice)*
> *Help, it's the bear! Run.... (retrace all of the actions back to the beginning)*
> *Phew! We're safe.*

- To complement this activity, your two-year-old may enjoy the book, *We're Going on a Bear Hunt* by Michael Rosen.

WHAT YOUR TWO-YEAR-OLD WILL LEARN:
Creativity

Five Little Monkeys

- This popular children's rhyme will delight your two-year-old, especially the part where she gets to shake her finger.

- Recite the poem and do the actions.

> *Five little monkeys (hold up five fingers)*
> *Jumping on the bed.*
> *One jumped off and*
> *Hurt his little head. (put your hand on your head and make*
> *a very sad face)*
> *Papa called the doctor, (pretend to dial a telephone)*
> *And the doctor said,*
> *"No more monkeys jumping on the bed!" (shake your index*
> *finger as you say the doctor's words)*

- Start the poem again with "Four little monkeys."

- Continue until there are no monkeys left.

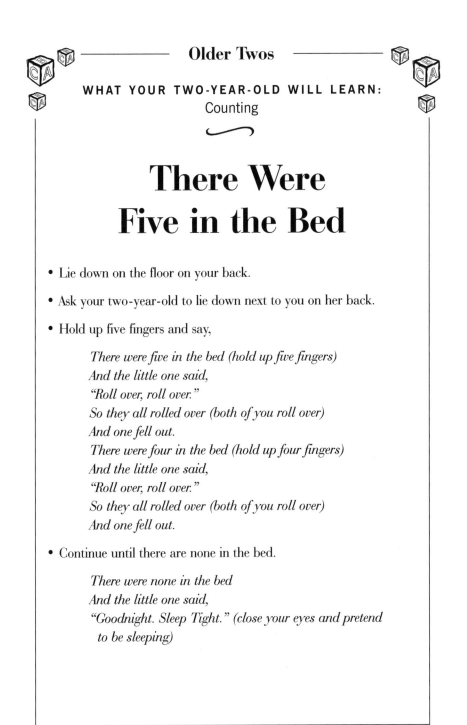

There Were Five in the Bed

- Lie down on the floor on your back.

- Ask your two-year-old to lie down next to you on her back.

- Hold up five fingers and say,

> *There were five in the bed (hold up five fingers)*
> *And the little one said,*
> *"Roll over, roll over."*
> *So they all rolled over (both of you roll over)*
> *And one fell out.*
> *There were four in the bed (hold up four fingers)*
> *And the little one said,*
> *"Roll over, roll over."*
> *So they all rolled over (both of you roll over)*
> *And one fell out.*

- Continue until there are none in the bed.

> *There were none in the bed*
> *And the little one said,*
> *"Goodnight. Sleep Tight." (close your eyes and pretend*
> *to be sleeping)*

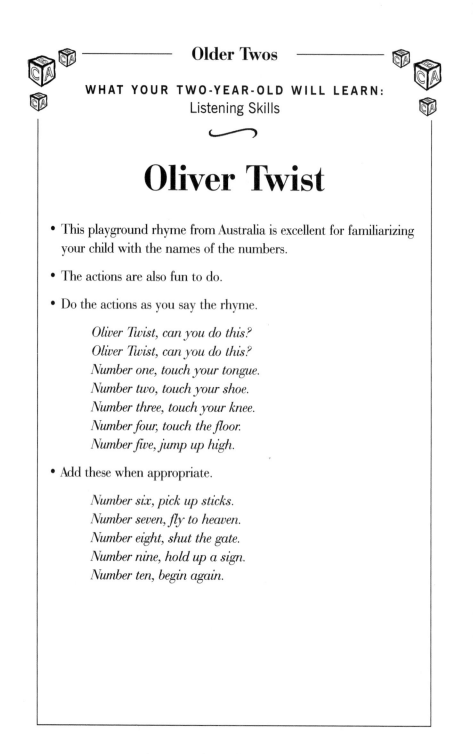

Oliver Twist

- This playground rhyme from Australia is excellent for familiarizing your child with the names of the numbers.

- The actions are also fun to do.

- Do the actions as you say the rhyme.

> *Oliver Twist, can you do this?*
> *Oliver Twist, can you do this?*
> *Number one, touch your tongue.*
> *Number two, touch your shoe.*
> *Number three, touch your knee.*
> *Number four, touch the floor.*
> *Number five, jump up high.*

- Add these when appropriate.

> *Number six, pick up sticks.*
> *Number seven, fly to heaven.*
> *Number eight, shut the gate.*
> *Number nine, hold up a sign.*
> *Number ten, begin again.*

Little Miss Muffet

- The nursery rhyme "Little Miss Muffet" is fun to act out.

- One person is "Miss Muffet" and the other is "the spider."

- Miss Muffet pretends that she is eating. When the spider comes next to her, she runs away.

- If your child is the spider, tell her to say, "Boo," and then you run away. This is very funny to a two-year-old.

    Little Miss Muffet sat on her tuffet,
    Eating her curds and whey.
    Along came a spider and sat down beside her,
    And frightened Miss Muffet away.

- Another way to play this game is to change the last line of the rhyme.

    Along came a spider and sat down beside her,
    And said, "What a very nice day!"

- Think of different things that the spider can say, such as, "Let's go play."

In and Out the Village

- The words of this song are sung to the tune of "Go In and Out the Window."

- Hold your child's hand. As you sing "Go in and out the village," run forward and backward.

    Go in and out the village,
    Go in and out the village,
    Go in and out the village,
    As you have done before. (clap your hands together)

- On the next part, reach up high and bend down low.

    Go up and down the village,
    Go up and down the village,
    Go up and down the village,
    As you have done before. (clap your hands together)

- This time walk around in a circle.

    Go round and round the village,
    Go round and round the village,
    Go round and round the village,
    As you have done before. (clap your hands together)

- Repeat the first verse.

AUTHOR'S NOTE: Whenever I play this game with two-year-olds, they want to do it over and over.

WHAT YOUR TWO-YEAR-OLD WILL LEARN:
Thinking Skills

Song Symbols

- Two-year-olds love to sing songs. They often hum and sing their favorite songs or make up their own songs.

- Find pictures and toys that go with her favorite songs. While she sings that song, hold that particular picture or toy. For example, if your child wants to sing "The Wheels on the Bus," hold a picture of a bus or hold a toy bus. Suggestions of songs and their toys include:
    - "Old MacDonald Had a Farm"—animal pictures or toys
    - "Twinkle, Twinkle Little Star"—pictures of stars and skies
    - "If You're Happy and You Know It"—smiling face pictures
    - "Hickory, Dickory Dock"—toy mouse, clock

- Reverse the procedure. Pick out a toy or picture and see if your little one knows what song it goes with.

WHAT YOUR TWO-YEAR-OLD WILL LEARN:
About Music

Fleas

- The words of this song follow the scale up and down. Think of how you would sing "do, re, mi, fa, sol, la, ti, do," and you can sing this song.

> *On my toe—DO*
> *There is a flea—RE*
> *Now he's climbing—MI*
> *On my knee—FA*
> *Past my tummy—SOL*
> *Past my nose—LA*
> *On my head where—TI*
> *My hair grows—DO*

- Now sing down the scale.

> *On my head there—DO*
> *Is a flea—TI*
> *Now he's climbing—LA*
> *Down on me—SOL*
> *Past my tummy—FA*
> *Past my knee—MI*
> *On my toe—RE*
> *Take that, you*
> *flea! (say the*
> *words and*
> *tickle your*
> *child's foot.)*

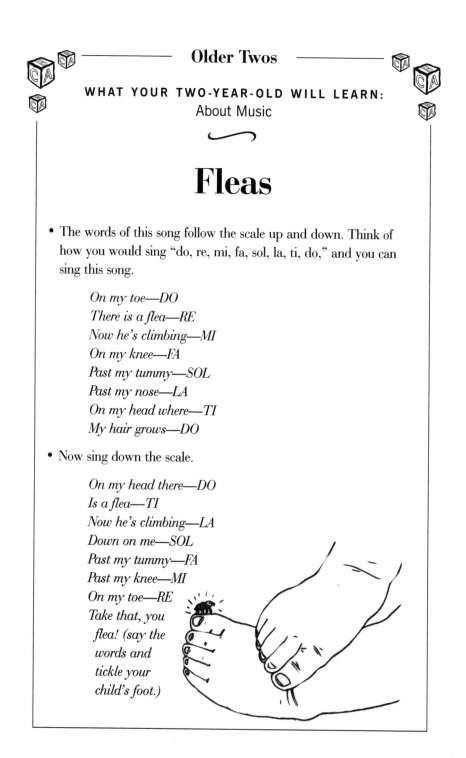

Jingle Bells

- Get small bells at a craft shop. Put two or three of these bells in a cardboard tube such as a paper towel tube. Tape the container closed.

- Sing the song and shake the bell shaker at the same time. Sing the song slowly and shake slowly. Sing the song fast and shake fast.

- Sing the song softly and loudly. The first part, which starts "Dashing through the snow," can be sung in a very soft voice. Sing the "jingle bells" part in a loud voice.

Jingle Bells

Dashing through the snow,
In a one-horse open sleigh,
O'er the fields we go,
Laughing all the way!

Bells on bobtail ring,
Making spirits bright,
What fun it is to ride and sing,
A sleighing song tonight!
Oh!

Jingle bells, jingle bells,
Jingle all the way.
Oh, what fun it is to ride,
In a one-horse open sleigh!

Jingle bells, jingle bells,
Jingle all the way.
Oh, what fun it is to ride,
In a one-horse open sleigh!

Let's Shake It

- Give your child two paper sacks and ask her to decorate them with markers.

- Partially fill the sacks with rice or beans and close them tightly with tape.

- Show your two-year-old how to shake the sacks to make sounds.

- Sing a favorite song while you accompany the song with the shakers.

- Play different kinds of music and dance around using the shakers.

- Sing this song to the tune of "Mary Had a Little Lamb" and perform the actions.

> *Shaker, shaker, up, up, up, (shake above your head)*
> *Down, down, down, (shake with hands down)*
> *Up, up, up, (shake above your head)*
> *Shaker, shaker all around,*
> *All around the town. (shake arms in a large circle)*

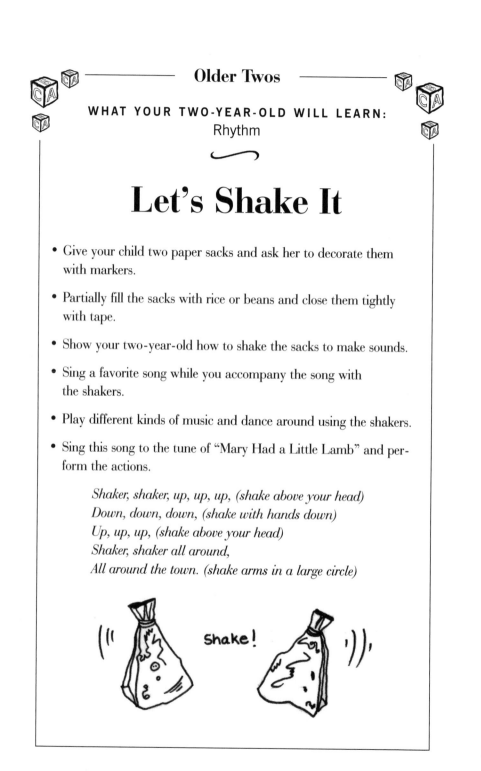

Who's That Singing?

- Two-year-olds enjoy listening to tapes.

- Choose one song that your child recognizes, for example, "Twinkle, Twinkle, Little Star."

- Invite members of your family to sing the song one at a time while you record them on a cassette tape. You can also have your child's friends or neighbors sing the song on the tape.

- Play the tape and see whether your child can recognize who is singing the song.

- Another tape to make is to ask different people to say positive things to your child, such as, "You sing beautifully," or "I like the things you make with blocks."

- Let your child listen to these affirmations as you ride in the car.

Telephone Fun

- Two-year-olds love to talk on the telephone, whether it's a real telephone or a pretend one.

- Get two play telephones, one for you and one for your two-year-old.

- Make up pretend conversations.

- When you begin, ask questions that only require a one-word answer.

  > *Adult:* Hello.
  > *Child:* Hello.
  > *Adult:* What is your name?
  > *Child:* My name is [child's name].

- Ask open-ended questions (use the "w" words—who, what, when, where, why) that require an answer. This develops your child's vocabulary.

- Another nice telephone game is to pretend to call people that your child knows. You make the call, and let your child be daddy, grandma, the dog, and so on. This will help your child think about answering the questions in different ways.

- Always end each conversation with "Goodbye."

WHAT YOUR TWO-YEAR-OLD WILL LEARN:
Imagination

Who's at the Door?

- Play a knock-at-the-door game with your two-year-old.

- Go into another room and close the door.

- Knock on the door. Your child says, " Who is it?" After waiting for the answer, she says, "Please come in."

- Now let your child do the knocking, and you say, "Who is it? Come in."

- Ask your child to pretend to be a dog. After you say, "Who is it? Come in," she opens the door and barks like a dog.

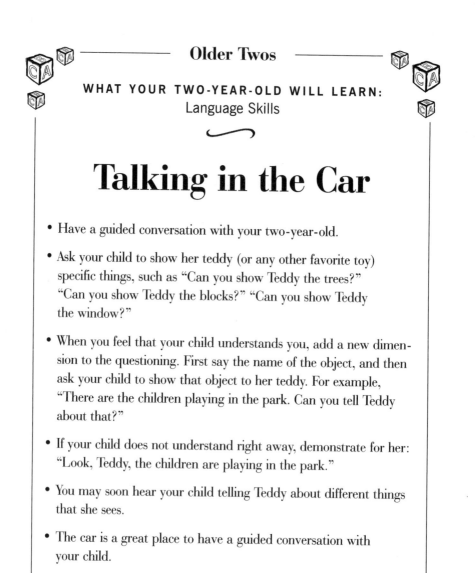

Talking in the Car

- Have a guided conversation with your two-year-old.

- Ask your child to show her teddy (or any other favorite toy) specific things, such as "Can you show Teddy the trees?" "Can you show Teddy the blocks?" "Can you show Teddy the window?"

- When you feel that your child understands you, add a new dimension to the questioning. First say the name of the object, and then ask your child to show that object to her teddy. For example, "There are the children playing in the park. Can you tell Teddy about that?"

- If your child does not understand right away, demonstrate for her: "Look, Teddy, the children are playing in the park."

- You may soon hear your child telling Teddy about different things that she sees.

- The car is a great place to have a guided conversation with your child.

Teddy Quiz

- Hold your child's teddy bear and ask it a question: "Are you a happy Teddy?"

- Move teddy's head up and down in a "yes" movement.

- Ask another question: "Is the sun shining outside?"

- Move teddy's head either "yes" or "no" depending on the weather.

- Give the teddy bear to your child and ask her to move the teddy's head to answer the questions.

- Ask questions that develop thinking skills. Here are some ideas.
    - Do dogs say meow?
    - What did you have for breakfast?
    - Where is the car?
    - How do you turn on the light?

- All these questions will encourage your child to think.

The Talking Room

- Ask a thought-provoking question, such as, "If you were a flower, what would you say?" Or, "If you were a chair, what would you say?"

- Thinking about something in a different way develops creative thinking.

- If your child is sitting in a chair, say, "Is this an elephant in the chair? Are you a lost little elephant?"

- Walk around the room with your two-year-old and talk to different objects.

- Ask questions of the objects and answer the questions in different voices.

  Hello chair, what's the matter?
  Chair: I want someone to sit on me.

  Hello flower, you are very beautiful.
  Flower: Please, please, smell me.

- This game is also excellent for developing language skills.

A Sound Story

- Making animal sounds is something that two-year-olds do very well.

- Make up a story using two animals. Ask your child to make the sound that animal makes each time you say the animal's name.

- Here is an example:

    Once upon a time there were two little doggies (Child makes a dog sound). They lived in a house with two cats (Child makes a cat sound)....

- Continue with the story, using each animal name three or four times.

- Once your child has learned this game, make up a new story with three animals or even four.

- This game will sharpen your child's listening skills.

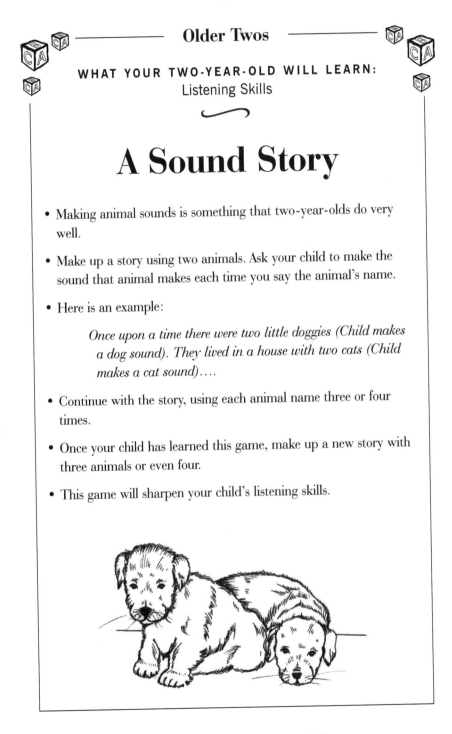

Games to Play with Two-Year-Olds

Acting Out a Story

- Older twos have certain books that they love, and they have enough language skills to say words from the book.

- Choose one of your child's favorite books and dramatize it. Start with a story that is simple and repetitious.

- A favorite is *Caps for Sale* by Esphyr Slobodkina. Children love to imitate the monkeys.

- Shake your finger at your child and say, "You monkeys, you, give me back my caps." Encourage your child to mimic you.

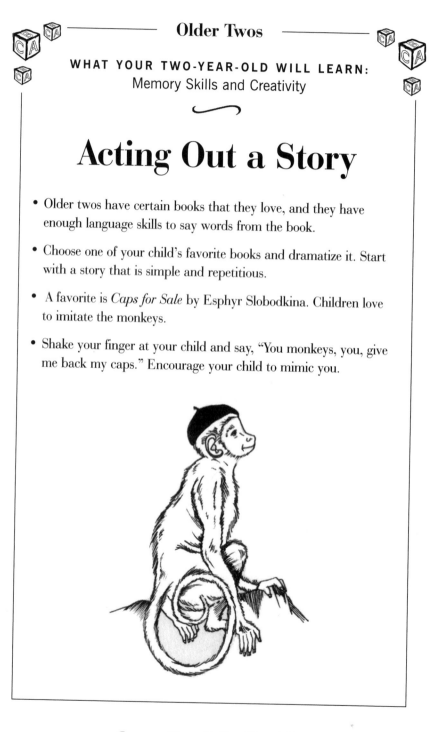

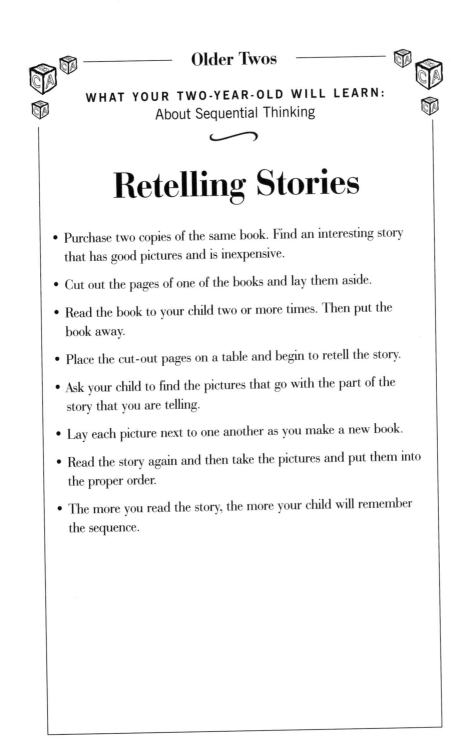

WHAT YOUR TWO-YEAR-OLD WILL LEARN:
About Sequential Thinking

Retelling Stories

- Purchase two copies of the same book. Find an interesting story that has good pictures and is inexpensive.

- Cut out the pages of one of the books and lay them aside.

- Read the book to your child two or more times. Then put the book away.

- Place the cut-out pages on a table and begin to retell the story.

- Ask your child to find the pictures that go with the part of the story that you are telling.

- Lay each picture next to one another as you make a new book.

- Read the story again and then take the pictures and put them into the proper order.

- The more you read the story, the more your child will remember the sequence.

Making Up Stories

- Put a few favorite toys into a basket.

- Ask your child to pick one of the toys from the basket.

- Make up a story about the toy that she picked.

- The story should be short and simple.

  Once upon a time there was a dog named Barney. He liked to jump up and down and wag his tail...

- This game will encourage your two-year-old to begin to make up stories with her toys.

The Thimble Family

- Using markers, paint faces on plastic thimbles.

- The faces can represent members of the family.

- Put one thimble on your finger and give another one to your child. Make up a conversation based on the thimble you are wearing.

- Ask questions that require a simple answer, for example, "Where are you going today?"

- Show your child how to move her finger as she "talks" for the thimble.

- Try changing voices for different thimble characters.

Puppet Talk

- Find a puppet that allows you to use your thumb, index, and middle fingers.

- Show your two-year-old all the different things that the puppet can do with its hands, such as clap, wave, and pat. Show your child what the puppet can do with its head such as nod, shake "yes," and shake "no."

- Ask the puppet questions, such as:
    - What do you like to eat?
    - What is your favorite toy?
    - Do you like to play outside?
    - Who is your friend?

- The puppet can ask your two-year-old questions. Use the questions above or additional questions, such as:
    - What is your favorite color?
    - Where are your feet?
    - What is your favorite book?
    - What does the cow say?

Wooden Spoon Puppets

- With a marker, draw a face on one side of a wooden spoon.

- Cut a slit in the middle of a scrap of material.

- Put the spoon handle through the slit and tape the material to the spoon so that it won't jiggle around.

- Give your two-year-old the spoon puppet and show her how to move it around, up and down, and back and forth.

- Encourage your child to make the puppet sing a song, read a story, or tell a story.

WHAT YOUR TWO-YEAR-OLD WILL LEARN:
Creativity

Snowman Sock

- Stuff a plain white sock with facial tissue.

- Tie it in three places to create a head and a two-part body.

- Give your two-year-old scraps of material so she can help decorate the puppet. Talk about what would make a good mouth, two eyes, and other features.

- When the puppet is finished, make up a simple story about a snowman. Try to use your child's name in the story.

Stuff a plain white sock with facial tissue.

Use scraps of material to decorate puppets.

Bunny Puppet

- Cut out a picture or draw a picture of a bunny's head.

- Tape the picture to the end of an ice cream stick.

- Poke a hole in the bottom of a paper cup and push the stick through the hole.

- The bunny's head should be sitting inside the cup. Your child can push the stick up and down to make the bunny pop out.

- Sing the song "Pop, Goes the Weasel," replacing the word "weasel" with "bunny." Encourage your child to pop the bunny up on the words "Pop, goes the bunny."

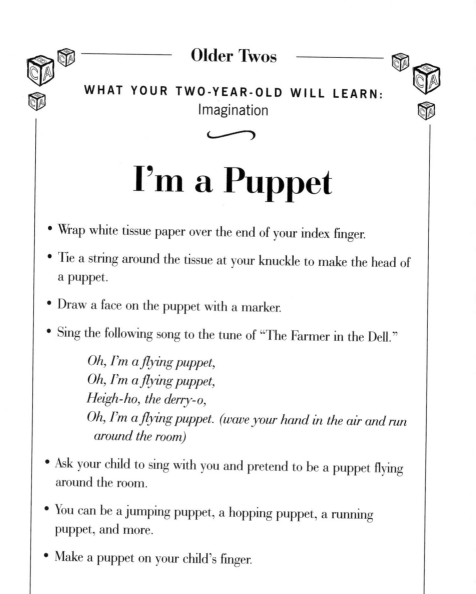

I'm a Puppet

- Wrap white tissue paper over the end of your index finger.

- Tie a string around the tissue at your knuckle to make the head of a puppet.

- Draw a face on the puppet with a marker.

- Sing the following song to the tune of "The Farmer in the Dell."

    Oh, I'm a flying puppet,
    Oh, I'm a flying puppet,
    Heigh-ho, the derry-o,
    Oh, I'm a flying puppet. (wave your hand in the air and run
        around the room)

- Ask your child to sing with you and pretend to be a puppet flying around the room.

- You can be a jumping puppet, a hopping puppet, a running puppet, and more.

- Make a puppet on your child's finger.

Easy Animal Puppets

- Look through magazines for pictures of animals. Let your child choose her favorite picture. It's best to use a picture that has one or two animals.

- Cut out the picture and tape it to a wooden spoon with a long handle. Voila! You have a puppet.

- Use a low table as a puppet stage and move the spoon around as you talk using your puppet.

- Start the conversation by asking your child questions that are simple for her to answer. For example, if you have a cow puppet, ask, "What does the cow say?" "Hello, would you like some milk?"

- Soon your little one will want to move the puppet and talk.

Tape cut-out picture onto the spoon

WHAT YOUR TWO-YEAR-OLD WILL LEARN:
Thinking Skills and Language Skills

Light On

- Hold your two-year-old so she can reach a wall switch.

- Say, "Light on," as she turns on the light.

- When the light is on, sing a favorite song such as "Mary Had a Little Lamb" or "Twinkle, Twinkle, Little Star."

- Say, "Light off" as she turns off the light.

- Put your fingers to your lips and say in a very soft voice, "Now it's time to be very quiet."

- Then say, "Light on" in a normal voice and play the game again.

- Soon your child will be saying the words for you.

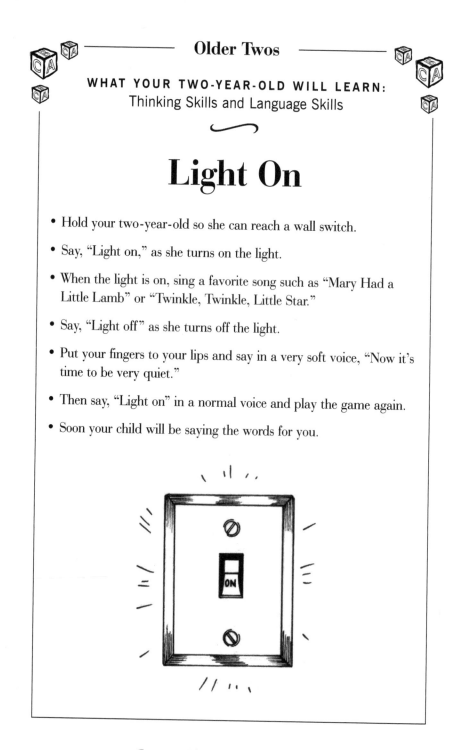

What Do You See?

- Sit on a chair or sofa with your two-year-old and her teddy bear.

- Say, "Teddy bear, teddy bear, what do you see?"

- Place the teddy bear on your nose.

- Say, "I see your nose, looking at me."

- Ask your child to take the teddy and put him on the table.

    Teddy bear, teddy bear,
    What do you see?
    I see the table looking at me.

- Soon your child will get the idea and begin to put the teddy bear in different places in the room or on her body.

- This game is a favorite with young children and readily develops their language.

- Your child also may enjoy Eric Carle's book, *Brown Bear, Brown Bear, What Do You See?*

I Spy

- You probably played this game when you were a child. This version is adapted for two-year-olds, and you will find that it really helps develop language skills.

- You will need a hollow tube, such as an empty paper towel tube, to look through, or use real binoculars.

- Look through the tube or binoculars and say:

  I spy with my little eye, something that is red.
  Is it the chair? No, it's not the chair.
  Is it the floor? No, it's not the floor.
  Is it a flower? Yes, it is a flower.

- Now let your child hold the binoculars and repeat the game.

- Encourage your child to say the words. After you say, "Is it the chair?" ask your child to say, "No, it's not the chair."

- She will probably say, "No" immediately and, as the game progresses, add more words.

- This is a humorous game for two-year-olds. They love to look for things that they recognize. For example, if you are looking for a teddy bear and you say, "Is it the door? No, it's not the door," your child will probably find it hilarious.

WHAT YOUR TWO-YEAR-OLD WILL LEARN:
Creativity and Imagination

Funny Stuff

- Two-year-olds are in the process of developing a sense of humor. They particularly enjoy calling something that they recognize by a different name.

- Pick out a favorite book and read it with your child.

- Look at the pictures and point to a picture and call it by a different name. For example, point to a dog and call it a "cat."

- They will think that is pretty funny and want you to do another one.

- Naming animals and body parts by the wrong name are very, very funny to a two-year-old.

- Call a nose an "ear." Call a toe a "finger."

Who's in the Picture?

- With your child, take pictures of familiar places such as the child's home, the street she lives on, a family pet, or her favorite stuffed animal. Be sure the child is in a lot of the pictures.

- Develop two copies of the pictures.

- Look through the pictures with your two-year-old and talk about each one. She will be delighted when she sees herself in the pictures.

- Pick out three pictures and place them in a pile.

- Give your child a picture that matches one of the three, and ask her to find the matching picture in the pile.

- When she matches the picture, praise her observation skills.

- Try this with another set of three pictures.

Same and Different

- Collect four pairs of things that are the same, such as silverware, blocks, paper cups, or mittens.

- Place all of the items on the floor and mix them up.

- Pick up one item and ask your little one to pick up another just like it.

- Continue picking up something and asking your child to find its match.

- Increase the difficulty by increasing the number of items to choose from.

- Each time your child finds the correct match, say, "Yes, that is the same."

WHAT YOUR TWO-YEAR-OLD WILL LEARN:
About Numbers

It's in the Cards

- Playing with cards is fun for two-year-olds.

- Looking at the cards, dropping them on the ground, and picking them up again will keep your child occupied for a long time.

- Play a pretend game of cards with your child.

- Deal out about ten cards, saying, "One for you and one for me." When all the cards are dealt, turn them over and talk about the pictures.

- Cut a slit in the top of a shoebox. Give your child cards to drop through the slit.

Pretty Red Card

- Take a few index cards and color one of them red.

- Hide the cards in different places in a room, such as under a chair or inside a drawer.

- Sing the following song to the tune of "Frere Jacque" or "Are You Sleeping?"

> *Pretty red card, pretty red card*
> *Where are you? Where are you?*
> *Where could you be hiding, where could you be hiding?*
> *Wish I knew, wish I knew.*

- Ask your child to find the red card. Give her a hint about where to find it. For example, "Can you find the red card under the chair?"

- After she finds the card, sing the song again.

- Repeat this game by hiding the card in other places or hiding a different colored card.

What Is Missing?

- Put two different toys on the floor.

- Ask your child to close her eyes, while you take one toy away.

- Then, ask her to open her eyes and guess which one is missing.

- Play the game at first using only two items. Later, to make the game harder, you may use more things.

- Ask your child to take things away for you to guess which one is gone.

- To extend this game, you could use two objects that are the same except for their color, such as a red block and a blue block, and take away one of the colored objects.

WHAT YOUR TWO-YEAR-OLD WILL LEARN:
Thinking Skills and Creativity

Animal Mix-Up

- Find pictures of several animals in magazines.

- Look at the pictures with your two-year-old and talk about how the animals look—are they furry, do they have four legs, are their noses big?

- Cut out the animal pictures and mount them on construction paper.

- Cut each animal picture into two pieces and mix up the pieces. Help your child match the pieces.

- Or mix up the pieces to invent new animals. For example, the head of a cat and a horse body could be called a "cathorse."

- What sound do think a "chickpig" would make?

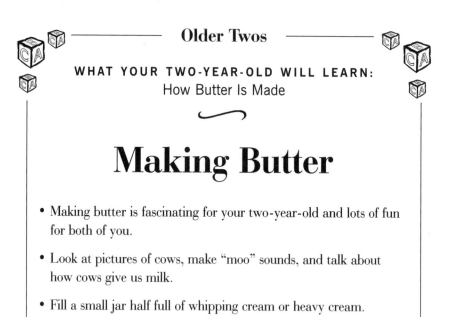

Making Butter

- Making butter is fascinating for your two-year-old and lots of fun for both of you.

- Look at pictures of cows, make "moo" sounds, and talk about how cows give us milk.

- Fill a small jar half full of whipping cream or heavy cream.

- Shake the jar vigorously. Let your child shake it, too.

- When you see the cream begin to separate, pour off the liquid or save it for baking.

- Continue shaking until a ball of butter is formed, then rinse the butter a few times, or until you see that the liquid is almost clear.

- As you rinse the butter, whip it with a spoon.

- Add salt to the butter and spread it on your favorite crackers.

The Bean Brigade

- There are so many kinds of beans in different colors, shapes, and sizes.

- Select several kinds and mix them together in a bowl.

- Help your two-year-old sort the beans into different groups. As you sort the beans, talk about the sizes, colors, and shapes.

- When all the beans have been sorted, wash them. Your child will enjoy doing this very much.

- Put them into a pot and cover them with water.

- Add a variety of vegetables and canned tomatoes. Let it cook until the beans are tender.

- Voila! Bean soup.

  CAUTION: Closely supervise the sorting and handling of beans by your two-year-old, especially if she still puts things into her mouth.

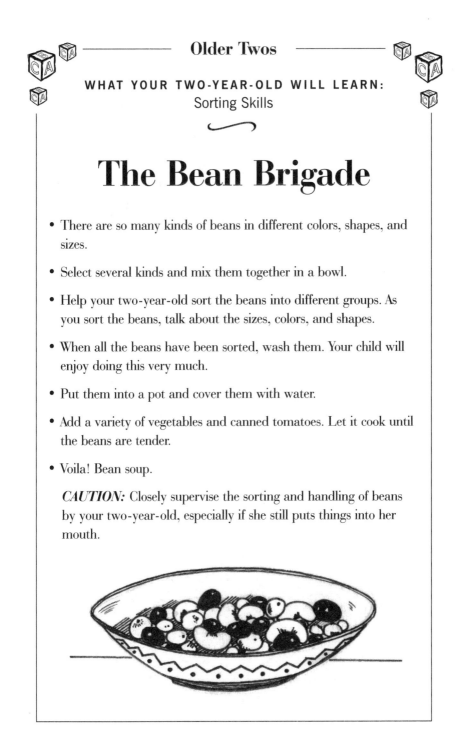

Pretend Party

- A pretend party for a two-year-old's imaginary friends or stuffed animals teaches counting, language, and social interaction skills.

- Gather together paper or plastic dishes, cups, and silverware.

- Decide how many friends you will be inviting to the party.

- Count out each item as you place it on the table.

- Serve cut-up fruit on each plate.

- Address each guest by name and ask her questions. For example,
    - Rabbit, do you like this fruit?
    - Doggie, what did you eat for breakfast?
    - Teddy, can you throw a ball?

- This kind of experience opens up a range of ideas to young minds.

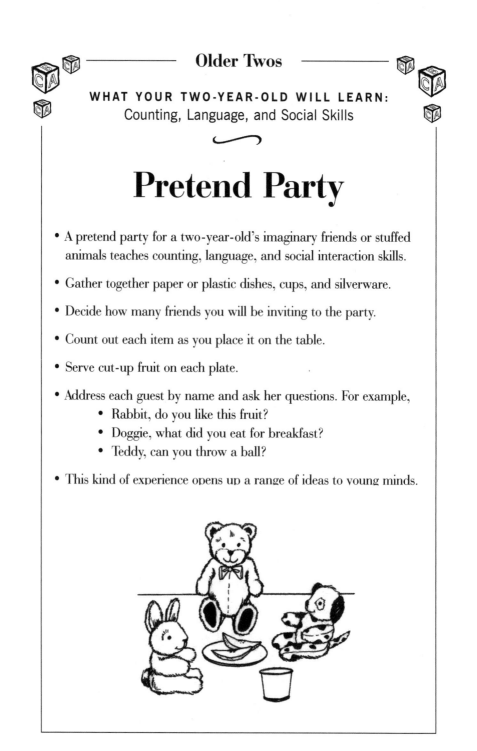

Teddy's Birthday

- Having a birthday party for teddy is good to do a week or two before your child's birthday. It gives you a chance to act out events that might happen at the real party.

- Two-year-olds love having parties for anybody, and their help in preparing teddy's party will make their own party more meaningful.

- Bring teddy and all his stuffed animal friends into one area or sit them in chairs at a table.

- Think about what you will be doing for your child's birthday and try to do the same things for teddy.
  - Make a birthday sign—"Happy Birthday, Teddy."
  - Put up festive decorations.
  - Play simple party games, such as Duck, Duck, Goose or Ring Around the Rosy.
  - Have gift-wrapped presents for teddy, such as a lollipop, a book, or a toy that your child can play with, too.

- You could even have a birthday cake.

- And don't forget to sing "Happy Birthday!"

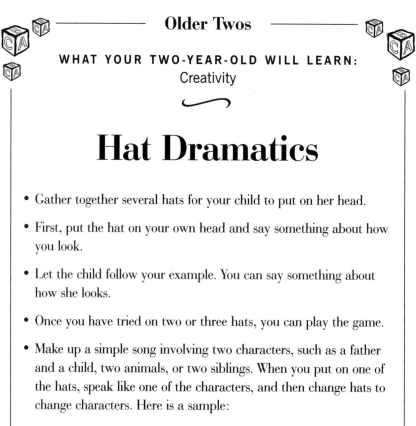

Hat Dramatics

- Gather together several hats for your child to put on her head.

- First, put the hat on your own head and say something about how you look.

- Let the child follow your example. You can say something about how she looks.

- Once you have tried on two or three hats, you can play the game.

- Make up a simple song involving two characters, such as a father and a child, two animals, or two siblings. When you put on one of the hats, speak like one of the characters, and then change hats to change characters. Here is a sample:

  First hat is mother: "What would you like to play today?"
  Second hat is child: "I want to play peek-a-boo!"

- Continue speaking for each character and changing hats each time.

- Stop the game when your child becomes tired of playing. This game requires a lot of thinking.

WHAT YOUR TWO-YEAR-OLD WILL LEARN:
Creativity

Paint Blobs

- This is a simple art game that is easy and fun for your two-year-old.

- Put dabs of tempera paint on a piece of white paper.

- The paper should be fairly sturdy, such as bond-quality copy paper.

- The more colors that you use, the more interesting the final product will be.

- Fold the paper in half.

- While the paper is still folded, encourage your child to "move" the paint around with her fingers.

- Open up the paper and look at the beautiful picture.

① Put dabs of paint on white paper.

② Fold the paper.

③ open paper up!

WHAT YOUR TWO-YEAR-OLD WILL LEARN:
About Shapes

Shape-agories

- This is a version of the game "Categories" for two-year-olds.

- Cut out a paper circle and show it to your child. Explain that today you are both going to look for round shapes.

- Throughout the day, point out circular shapes, such as a round sign, round knobs, tires on cars, doorknobs, or a ball.

- When you feel that your child is beginning to understand what a circle is, play the game with a new shape.

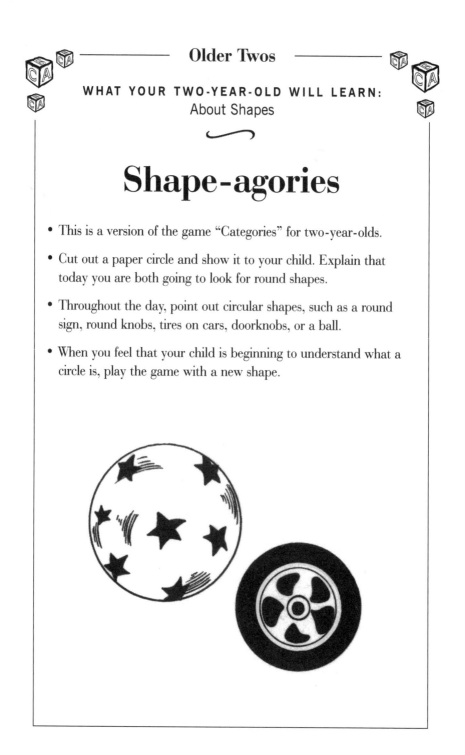

Making Designs

- Think about all the ways that you can make a circle:
    - With your thumb and index finger
    - With your arms
    - With blocks
    - By tracing around circular objects (a bowl, a cup)
    - By drawing circles of different sizes with a crayon
    - By placing your child in the middle of a circle of stuffed animals

- Each time you make a circle, say, "Circle" to your two-year-old. Look for circles in your house, in the yard, or wherever you go.

- Give your child a large piece of drawing paper and a crayon and guide her hand to make circles. Hold circular objects on the paper and guide her hand to draw around them.

Shape Up

- Two-year-olds are beginning to understand different shapes.

- Give your child two index cards that have been cut into different shapes, such as one circle card and one square card.

- Use a different color crayon to color each shape.

- Sing the song "Where is Thumbkin" and change the words to "Where's the circle…" As you sing "Where is the circle, here I am," hold up the circle shape.

- For each verse, focus on a color or a shape and hold up the appropriate color or shape with each verse.

- Serve crackers in a variety of different shapes and talk about the shapes.

Red, Green, Yellow

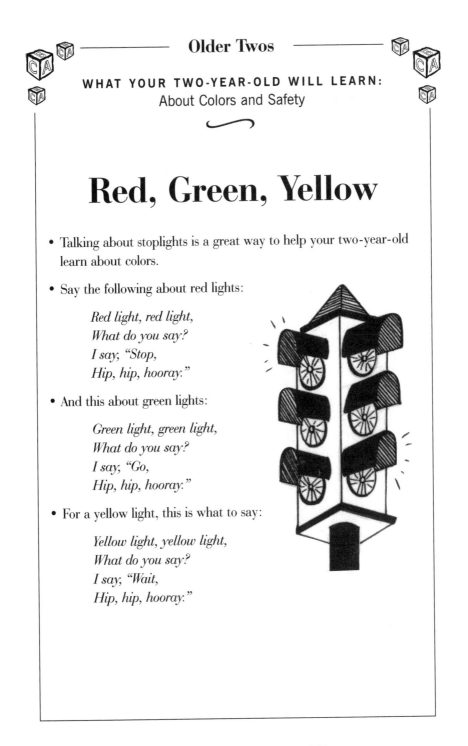

- Talking about stoplights is a great way to help your two-year-old learn about colors.

- Say the following about red lights:

  Red light, red light,
  What do you say?
  I say, "Stop,
  Hip, hip, hooray."

- And this about green lights:

  Green light, green light,
  What do you say?
  I say, "Go,
  Hip, hip, hooray."

- For a yellow light, this is what to say:

  Yellow light, yellow light,
  What do you say?
  I say, "Wait,
  Hip, hip, hooray."

Red Food

- Older two-year-olds love to learn about colors.

- Your child can help you prepare red foods while at the same time, learn their names and how they taste.

- Tomato juice and cranberry juice are very tasty. Let your child pour the juice for a snack.

- Tomatoes are delicious, and your child can help wash them.

- Many fruits are red, such as apples, strawberries, plums, and cherries. Your child can help wash and arrange them on a plate.

CAUTION: You might want to pit the cherries before your child eats them.

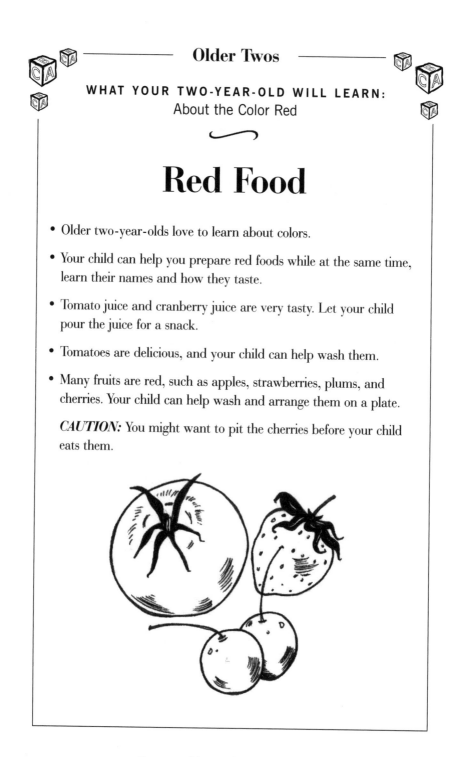

Ones and Twos

- Saying the words "one" and "two," and being able to hold up one or two fingers, does not necessarily mean that a two-year-old understands the concepts.

- Experiencing numbers using all her senses will help your child acquire that understanding.

- Begin by talking about "a lot," "a few" and "one."

- Assemble blocks in groups of seven, three, and one.

- Talk with your child about which group has a lot of blocks, a few blocks, and one block.

- Ask your child to give you a block.

- Continue placing other objects in groups of a few, a lot, and one. Stuffed animals and rocks are fun to use.

- Each time, ask your child to give you one item.

- When you think that your child understands the concept of "one," begin introducing the concept of "two": two socks, two shoes, two hands, two eyes, and so on.

- Play the same game, always including a group of "two."

Chalk Numbers

- Write the numbers 0 through 10 in large print on the sidewalk.

- Use colored chalk, alternating the colors so that your two-year-old will see where one number ends and the next begins.

- Hold your child's hand and walk on the numbers. Say the name of each number as you step on it.

- Let her try this by herself. You say the numbers, and she does the walking.

- If she walks slowly, say the numbers slowly.

- If she walks fast, say the numbers fast.

- You can also write the letters of the alphabet or the names of everyone in the family.

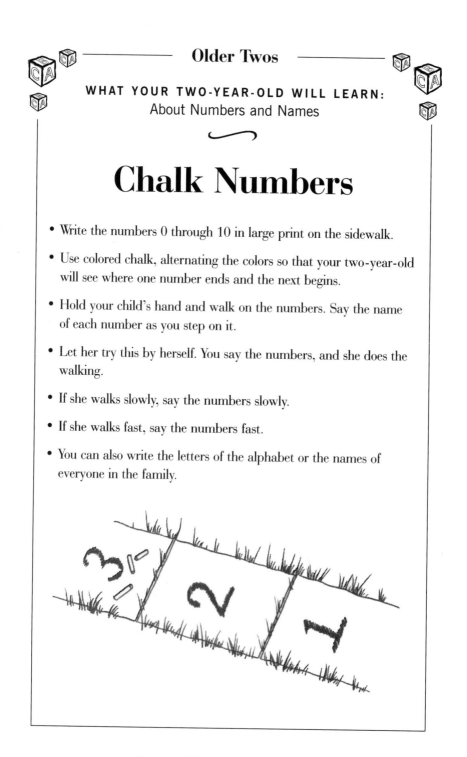

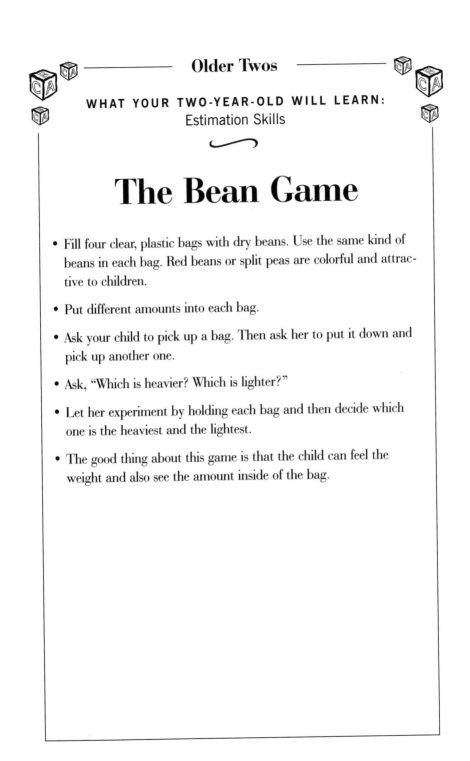

The Bean Game

- Fill four clear, plastic bags with dry beans. Use the same kind of beans in each bag. Red beans or split peas are colorful and attractive to children.

- Put different amounts into each bag.

- Ask your child to pick up a bag. Then ask her to put it down and pick up another one.

- Ask, "Which is heavier? Which is lighter?"

- Let her experiment by holding each bag and then decide which one is the heaviest and the lightest.

- The good thing about this game is that the child can feel the weight and also see the amount inside of the bag.

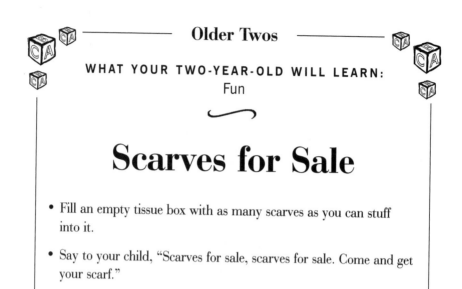

Scarves for Sale

- Fill an empty tissue box with as many scarves as you can stuff into it.

- Say to your child, "Scarves for sale, scarves for sale. Come and get your scarf."

- Let your child pull one scarf out of the box. Show her how to dance around the room with the scarf.

- Repeat "Scarves for sale," and let her pull out the next scarf. Encourage her to dance around the room again.

- When all the scarves have been pulled out of the box, ask your two-year-old to put them back into the box. She will love doing this.

- As each scarf is pulled out of the box, tell your two-year-old what color it is.

Fascinating Bugs

- Show your two-year-old pictures of bugs such as flies, bees, and spiders.

- Go outside and section off a small area by drawing in the dirt with a stick.

- Look closely within that area to see if anything is moving.

- Give your child a magnifying glass to look for bugs.

- You will be amazed at what you will see.

- Take the magnifying glass to another part of the yard and repeat the game.

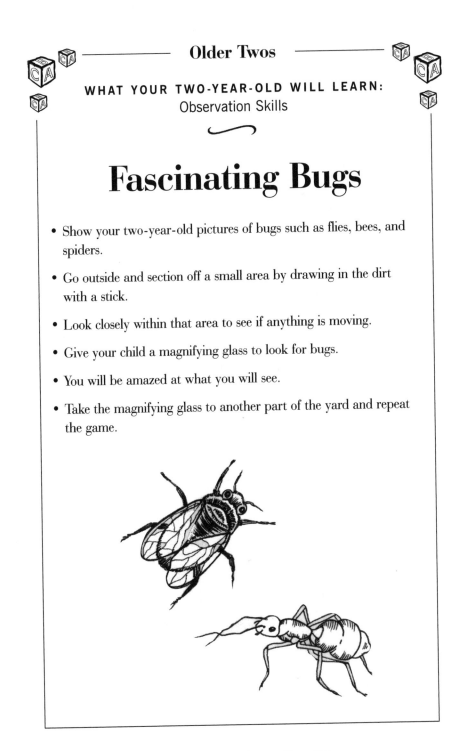

Games to Play with Two-Year-Olds

Outside Creatures

- Take your two-year-old on a walk outdoors and look for animals and insects.

- When you see a squirrel or a chipmunk, talk about how they move. Try to imitate their movements.

- Look for clues that an animal has been around. Holes in the ground and footprints in the dirt are good signs.

- Listen to the sounds of the birds and see whether you can figure out from the sounds where they are.

- Look for bird nests and squirrel nests in the trees.

- Sit together and feel the air on your faces and smell the wonderful aromas of the outdoors.

WHAT YOUR TWO-YEAR-OLD WILL LEARN:
About Growing

Little Flower

- Plant seeds in two pots. Put one pot in full sun and give the other no sun at all.

- Water the pots each day.

- As the plants grow, your child will begin to understand that sunshine is important for growth.

- Repeat the experiment, but place both pots in full sun. This time water only one pot. Again, your two-year-old will see a dramatic example that water is important for growth.

- Look at the flowers outside and talk about how once they were tiny seeds, and now they are beautiful flowers.

WHAT YOUR TWO-YEAR-OLD WILL LEARN:
About Same and Different

Nature Trip

- Select a few items from outside, such as a small rock, a flower, a twig, or an acorn.

- Talk about the items with your child. Let her hold them as you talk about the texture and the color.

- Now, go into the yard and search for a matching item. Guide your child to the area where you found the flower or acorn and encourage her to discover a matching flower or acorn.

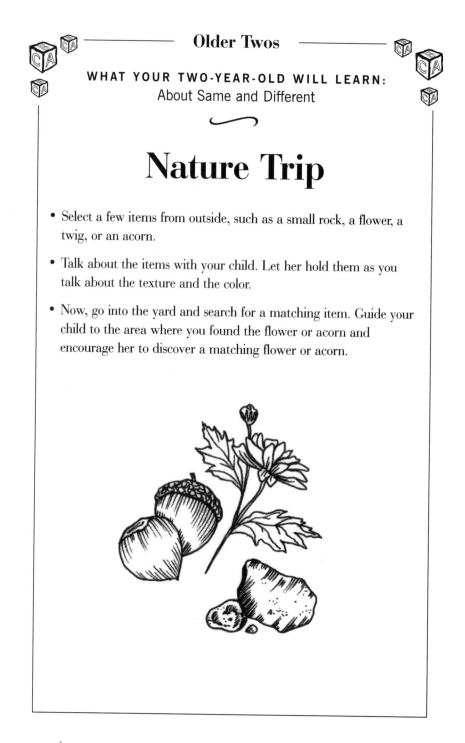

What's in the Box?

- This is a wonderful thinking game.

- Go outside with your two-year-old and collect familiar objects such as leaves, rocks, acorns, or a flower.

- Place the objects on the ground and talk about them. Say their names and something about them, for example, "The leaves are from the trees."

- Take three items and put them into a box that you have brought outdoors. A shoebox works well.

- As you place articles in the box, repeat their names. You might ask your two-year-old to put them into the box.

- Ask your child to cover her eyes as you say:

  Open the door, open the locks,
  I will take something out of the box.

- Remove one item. See if your child can tell you what is missing from the box.

- As your two-year-old plays this game, you can put more things into the box. You can even remove two items at a time.

Starlight

- Take a blanket outside on a warm evening, lie down, and look at the sky.

- Talk about what you see, such as the moon, the stars, the planets, or airplanes.

- Your two-year-old will enjoy looking at the sky and spending this time with you. Help her to imagine astronauts on the moon.

- Explain what the word "wish" means and teach her to wish on the first star.

  Starlight, star bright,
  First star I see tonight,
  I wish I may, I wish I might,
  Have this wish I wish tonight.

- This is also the perfect time to sing "Twinkle, Twinkle, Little Star."

  Twinkle, twinkle, little star,
  How I wonder what you are.
  Up above the earth so high,
  Like a diamond in the sky,
  Twinkle, twinkle, little star,
  How I wonder what you are.

Let's Think About...

- Sit on a soft chair or sofa with your child next to you or in your lap.

- Say, "Let's think about a sleeping kitten."

- Pretend to be asleep and talk very softly.

- Then say, "Let's think about the little fish in the water. They are so quiet as they swim."

- Pretend to be a little fish in the water.

- Tell your two-year-old that when she gets angry, she can think about the sleeping kitten or the little fish.

- To reinforce these skills, pretend to be these animals again.

Games to Play with Two-Year-Olds

WHAT YOUR TWO-YEAR-OLD WILL LEARN:
Creativity

Taking Trips

- Taking your two-year-old to a variety of places will develop her vocabulary.

- Each time you go to a different place, talk about it before and after the trip.

- Draw pictures about what you saw on your trip and find books about the place that you visited.

- Suggestions of places to visit are the fire station, the police station, the airport, the train station, an apple orchard, a farm, or the zoo.

- Hang a bulletin board or a large chart on a wall in your child's room. Each time you visit a new place, put a picture of that place on the chart. This will give you a chance to remember where you visited.

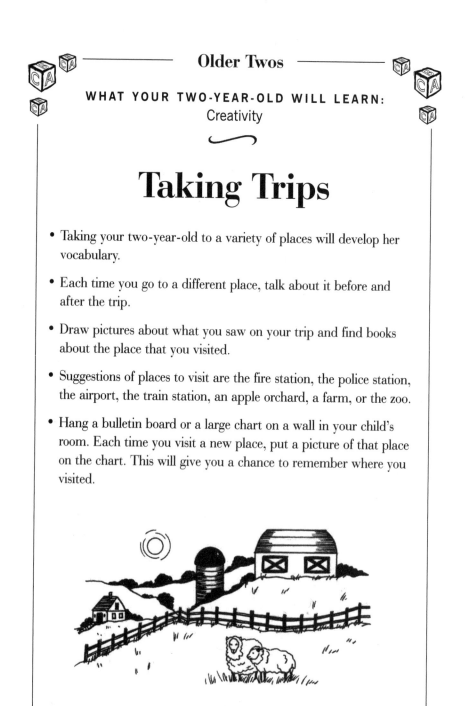

Index